Attacks on the Press

The Committee to Protect Journalists is an independent, nonprofit organization that promotes press freedom worldwide, defending the right of journalists to report the news without fear of reprisal. CPJ ensures the free flow of news and commentary by taking action wherever journalists are attacked, imprisoned, killed, kidnapped, threatened, censored or harassed.

Attacks on the Press

2017 EDITION

The New Face of Censorship

Committee to Protect Journalists

WILEY | Bloomberg
PRESS

Cover photo: Supporters gather to rally with Donald Trump, then the Republican presidential nominee, in a cargo hangar at Minneapolis–Saint Paul International Airport in Minneapolis, Minnesota, on November 6, 2016. (REUTERS/Jonathan Ernst)

Editor: Alan Huffman
Editorial Director: Elana Beiser
Copy Editor: April Simpson

For general information on our other products and services or for technical support, please contact our Customer Care Department within the United States at (800) 762-2974, outside the United States at (317) 572-3993 or fax (317) 572-4002.

Wiley publishes in a variety of print and electronic formats and by print-on-demand. Some material included with standard print versions of this book may not be included in e-books or in print-on-demand. If this book refers to media such as a CD or DVD that is not included in the version you purchased, you may download this material at http://booksupport.wiley.com. For more information about Wiley products, visit www.wiley.com.

Library of Congress Cataloging-in-Publication Data:

ISBN 9781119361008 (Paperback)
ISBN 9781119361015 (ePDF)
ISBN 9781119361060 (ePub)

Printed in the United States of America

10 9 8 7 6 5 4 3 2 1

MIX
Paper from
responsible sources
FSC
www.fsc.org
FSC® C132124

Contents

Introduction: The New Face of Censorship

By Joel Simon

I n the days when news was printed on paper, censorship was a crude practice involving government officials with black pens, the seizure of printing presses and raids on newsrooms. The complexity and centralization of broadcasting also made radio and television vulnerable to censorship even when the governments didn't exercise direct control of the airwaves. After all, frequencies can be withheld; equipment can be confiscated; media owners can be pressured.

New information technologies—the global, interconnected internet; ubiquitous social media platforms; smartphones with cameras—were supposed to make censorship obsolete. Instead, they have just made it more complicated.

Does anyone still believe the utopian mantras that information wants to be free and the internet is impossible to censor or control?

The fact is that while we are awash in information, there are tremendous gaps in our knowledge of the world. The gaps are growing as violent attacks against the media spike, as governments develop new systems of information control and as the technology that allows information to circulate is co-opted and used to stifle free expression.

In 2014, I published a book about the global press freedom struggles, *The New Censorship*. In this year's edition of *Attacks on the Press*, we have asked contributors from around the world—journalists, academics and activists—to provide their perspectives on the issue. The question we have asked them to answer—with apologies to Donald Rumsfeld—is why don't we know what we don't know.

Following the polarizing election of Donald Trump in the United States, concerns were raised about the rise of fake news and the hostile and intimidating environment created by Trump's heated rhetoric. But around the world, the trends are deeper, more enduring and more troubling. These days, the strategies to control and manage information fall into three broad categories that I call repression 2.0, masked political control and technology capture.

Repression 2.0 is an update on the worst old-style tactics, from state censorship to the imprisonment of critics, with new information technologies, including smartphones and social media, producing a softening around the edges. Masked political control means a systematic effort to hide repressive actions by dressing them in the cloak of democratic norms. Governments might justify an internet crackdown by saying it is necessary to suppress hate speech and incitement to violence. They might cast the jailing of dozens of critical journalists as an essential element in the global fight against terror.

Finally, technology capture means using the same technologies that have spawned the global information explosion to stifle dissent by monitoring and surveilling critics, blocking websites and using trolling to shut down critical voices. Most insidious of all is sowing confusion through propaganda and false news.

These strategies have contributed to an upsurge in killings and imprisonment of journalists around the world. In fact, at the end of 2016, there were 259 journalists in jail, the most ever documented by the Committee to Protect Journalists (CPJ). Meanwhile, violent forces—from Islamic militants to drug cartels—have exploited new information technologies to bypass the media and communicate directly with the public, often using videos of graphic violence to send a message of ruthlessness and terror.

In his essay, CPJ's deputy executive director, Robert Mahoney, describes the global safety landscape and looks at the ways that journalists and media organizations are responding to these troubling trends. The threat of violence is stifling coverage of critical global hot spots from Syria to Somalia to the U.S.-Mexico border, creating a dangerous information void.

Two essays describe strategies journalists are using to respond. As a reporter for the AP based in Senegal, Rukmini Callimachi worked the phones to cover the no-go zones in neighboring Mali, developing sources and an intimate knowledge of the country that allowed her to provide rich, informed coverage once she was able to get in on the ground. Callimachi replicated these efforts to cover terror networks around the world as a reporter for *The New York Times*. Similarly, *Syria Deeply* managing editor Alessandria Masi has covered every aspect of the Syrian conflict without ever setting foot inside the country.

The new technologies that allow criminal and militant groups to bypass the media and speak directly to the public have made the world exceptionally dangerous for journalists reporting from conflict zones. But this same process of disintermediation poses challenges to authoritarian regimes around the world that in the past have often managed information through direct control of mass media. Popular movements—from the Color Revolutions to the Arab Spring—have been fueled by information shared on social media, and because anyone with a smartphone can commit acts of journalism, it's impossible to jail them all.

Finding the balance between the repressive force necessary to retain control and the openness necessary to benefit from new technologies and participate in the global economy is an ongoing challenge for authoritarian regimes. As Jessica Jerreat notes, in North Korea modest cracks are emerging in the wall of censorship with the opening of an AP bureau and the growing use of cell phones, even if these phones are monitored and controlled. In Cuba, a new generation of bloggers and online journalists criticize the socialist government from a variety of perspectives, and although they face the prospects of harassment and persecution, they are not subject to the mass jailing of journalists in the previous decade.

Outside the world's more repressive countries, governments generally seek to hide their repression behind a democratic veneer. In his book *The Dictator's Learning Curve*, William J. Dobson describes how a generation of autocratic leaders uses the trappings of democracy, including elections, to mask their repression. I have dubbed these elected autocrats *democratators*.

President Recep Tayyip Erdoğan of Turkey is perhaps an exemplar, and while his country jails more journalists than any other, Andrew Finkel shows in his essay how Erdoğan's government also exercises control over the private media using direct pressure, regulatory authority and the law as a blunt instrument to ensure obeisance. Likewise, in Egypt, which has seen a massive upsurge in repression, the government of President Abdel Fattah el-Sisi has expended considerable energy and effort to build a loyal press.

In Mexico, a country that has experienced a democratic transition, an infamous, near-perfect record of impunity in the murders of journalists, coupled with the manipulation of government advertising and strategic lawsuits, has cast a chill over the country's media, according to *New York Times* correspondent Elisabeth Malkin. As Alan Rusbridger notes in his detailed report on the Kenyan media scene, "Murder is messy. Money is tidy."

These strategies focus on political control and manipulation. But, of course, governments also seek to capture the technology that journalists and others rely on to disseminate critical information. These same technologies can be used for surveillance, blocking, trolling and the dissemination of propaganda. In her essay, Emily Parker contrasts the approaches of China and Russia, noting that Russia failed to grasp early on the political threat posed by the World Wide Web and thus has been playing catch-up. Today, even as Russia struggles to curtail online dissent, it is developing what could be termed *offensive capabilities*, using the internet to spread propaganda and manipulate public opinion domestically and around the world.

Other governments, including China, are also innovating. One of the most dramatic and disturbing examples is the development of a tracking system based on credit scores. As described by Yaqiu Wang, Chinese journalists who post critical content on social media could receive poor credits scores, resulting in the denial of loans or high interest rates. The government of Ecuador, according to Alexandra Ellerbeck, is alleging copyright and terms of service violations in pressuring Twitter and Facebook to remove links to sensitive documents that expose corruption. Meanwhile, governments, including of the United States, are promoting the concept of transparency by releasing reams of data, which, while welcome, are often of limited utility. And journalists who file freedom of information requests face impediments ranging from delaying tactics to exorbitant fees.

As with any book, and particularly one of this nature, a lot will have changed by the time this edition of *Attacks on the Press* comes out. Circumstances are extraordinarily volatile around the world, including in the United States, as Christiane Amanpour and Alan Huffman note in their chapters. Overall, the landscape of new censorship is bleak, and the challenges significant. The enemies of free expression have attacked the new global information system at every level, using violence and repression against individual journalists, seeking to control the technologies on which they rely to deliver the news, and sowing confusion and disinformation so that critical information does not reach the public in a meaningful way.

But the fight is far from hopeless. It is important to keep in mind that the upsurge in violence and repression against the media, and the development of new strategies of repression, are responses to the liberating power of independent information. Technology continues to serve the voices of critical dissent, as Karen Coates describes in her essay on Facebook journalism.

Journalists cannot allow themselves to feel demoralized. They need to pursue their calling and to seek the truth with integrity, honestly believing that the setbacks, while real, are temporary. As Amanpour argues in the closing essay in this volume (adapted from a speech she gave at the CPJ awards dinner in November 2016), journalists must "recommit to robust fact-based reporting without fear or favor—on the issues" and not "stand for being labeled crooked or lying or failing." This is the best and most important way to fight back against the new censorship.

Joel Simon is the executive director of the Committee to Protect Journalists. He has written widely on media issues, contributing to Slate, Columbia Journalism Review, The New York Review of Books, World Policy Journal, Asahi Shimbun *and* The Times of India. *He has led numerous international missions to advance press freedom. His book* The New Censorship: Inside the Global Battle for Media Freedom *was published in November 2014.*

1. Where I've Never Set Foot

By Alessandria Masi

Syrian children react after what activists said was shelling by forces loyal to President Bashar al-Assad near the Syrian Arab Red Crescent center in Damascus on May 6, 2015.

(Reuters/Bassam Khabieh)

The morning after the attack my deputy editor and I lit ciga-
rettes as we squatted on the green couch in our closet-sized
Beirut office, hanging out the window and talking about what
we thought had really happened in Syria.

Here were the facts: On September 17, 2016, the U.S. and several
coalition partners had launched several air strikes on a Syrian military
base in the province of Deir Ezzor, in eastern Syria, killing 62 soldiers.
Syria, at that point, had been on the sixth day of a cease-fire, brokered
the week before by U.S. and Russian officials, but the situation was bad.
The following days in Syria were some of the bloodiest since the start
of the conflict in 2011.

Our news site, *Syria Deeply*, had already published a report on
the attack—mostly bare-bones facts and whatever official statements
had been issued by all concerned. We included the official U.S. statement confirming the strike, saying it was an accident. We reported that
the United Nations immediately convened an emergency session in
an attempt to salvage the already shaky truce. We even reported that
Moscow, enraged, said the attack was proof that the U.S. was coordi-
nating with the so-called Islamic State group (IS, or ISIS; the group's
militants were apparently able to advance in the area just minutes after
the air strike). These were statements released to the press, to be used
by the press to transmit information to the public. But you would be
hard-pressed to find anyone, including the two of us, who believed that
all three statements were true.

To me, it seemed an insult to the public's intelligence for us to
report that the U.S. was not able to recognize a military base. I am
wary of believing anything President Bashar al-Assad says but had to
concede that he wasn't completely wrong in pointing out that "you
don't commit a mistake for more than one hour." Yet I've also been
privy to U.S. strategy long enough to know that direct coordination
between Washington and ISIS would be an unnecessary risk when
there were plenty of willing middlemen at both parties' disposal, and it
seemed unlikely that the U.S. would willingly obliterate its own cease-
fire deal.

A few days later, over wine and Armenian food on my balcony
in Beirut, another journalist shared that a prominent NGO (nongovernmental organization) spokesperson blamed the attack on Russia,

saying Moscow had cleared the target with the Americans before the strike.

None of these possibilities made it into the news brief. It's not because we too were lazy to confirm our theories, nor because we didn't have the sources or lacked understanding of Syria. Six years into the conflict that has killed hundreds of thousands of people, flooded other countries with nearly 4.8 million refugees and drawn in foreign powers from all corners of the world, journalists reporting on Syria must censor themselves through omission. This isn't new—covering Syria has always involved a certain amount of self-censorship, either for security reasons (names are always changed) or for ethical reasons (we omit pictures of the dead). But now, ironically, we do it to try to remain unbiased. We walk on eggshells for the sake of balance and because the majority of us cannot go to Syria to see things for ourselves, which means we are forced to report only what we are told.

As a journalist and managing editor of *Syria Deeply*, I realized that omitting our theories and reporting only those questionable statements accomplished two things: Readers were informed that the strike happened, and, as a publication, we left very little room for accusations of bias. We reported all sides' statements.

I have a recurring nightmare about Syria. I wake up one day, when the war is over, to find that all the information we reported as fact—everything we thought was true—was not. It's an irrational thought. As I write this, the conflict has claimed the lives of some 400,000 people, families have been torn apart, cities have been destroyed, multitudes have fled (and often perished), overwhelming other countries, and millions of Syrians don't know where they will get their next meal. Those are undeniable facts. The war is taking a huge toll. But I haven't seen it myself, and there are few people I trust to be my eyes on the ground, because after six years of fighting, the agenda-less are a minuscule percentage of the Syrian population. Government statements are often blatantly misleading, and fear of retribution from government or non-state actors leads civilians and activists to bend or sometimes obliterate the truth. For those of us covering the conflict from the outside, it is hard to know what's really happening, so we either self-censor or grudgingly provide a platform for people whose accounts may be wildly divergent or entirely untrue.

When Russia first began its air campaign in Syria in October 2015, I was in Beirut. As the first reports of the strike came out, I called a Syrian source in the town that was hit, who provided me with recordings of intercepted radio communications in Russian coming from the warplanes. Moscow had already put out their statement claiming to have joined the war in Syria under the pretense of fighting ISIS. But looking at my map of Syria, I found the first town that had been hit circled in red—it had been under siege for more than a year and was under the control of a Syrian rebel group, not ISIS.

My editors in New York were skeptical. "Why would Russia bomb the rebels when they have explicitly said they are bombing ISIS?" they asked. "It doesn't make sense." The majority of news outlets had already published the Russian government statement about their fight against ISIS, and I was contradicting this. My sources were part of the opposition and because of their affiliation I had to be cautious; they had every reason to lie.

In the days that followed, it became common knowledge that regardless of Moscow's official statement, Russia was in Syria to defend Assad, and this meant targeting any group that opposed him, including the rebels. Yet we continued to include the official Moscow statement in our reporting.

Politicians have always lied, and it has always been the responsibility of journalists to filter these statements or juxtapose them with evidence proving them false. But in Syria, even evidence is presented subjectively, and obtaining your own eyewitness account can mean jail or a death sentence.

So we choose to err on the safe side, which often sounds like this:

Russian air strikes hit a hospital in Aleppo, though Moscow claims it is fighting ISIS in Syria.

Air strikes hit a school in Syria. It is unclear who carried out the attack— Syria, Russia and the U.S.-led coalition (the only players with air power in the country) all denied involvement.

Patrick Cockburn wrote in his book *The Age of Jihad*, "Media reporting has been full of certainties that melt away in the face of reality. In Syria, more than most places, only eyewitness information is worth much." It is this that worries me the most. I have seen thousands of photos, videos and reports. I have spoken to dozens of people inside. I have Skyped with activists, detainees and victims. I have gone to conferences. I have met with advocacy groups and tracked the work of humanitarian aid organizations. I have been a secondhand witness to the war and reported closely on it, yet I have never set foot in Syria. Admitting this has given me much anxiety over being labeled a fraud, but it's the truth, as it is for many international journalists covering the war.

In the early years of the war, when foreign journalists were going into Syria frequently, some with government visas and others crossing the border illegally, I was still in university. When it was finally my turn to cover the war in 2014, journalists were being targeted. The Committee to Protect Journalists estimates that more than 100 journalists have been killed since the start of the conflict. As a direct consequence, coverage has become constricted, most often limited to secondhand accounts.

Today, there are dozens of Syrian journalists still inside the country risking their lives to report the news. (CPJ investigated the deaths of at least 90 in 2015 but was only able to confirm that 14 were killed that year because of their work.) However, most are confined to either opposition-held or government-held areas and cannot cross front lines for their work. Some are able to publish their own work on local and international media outlets, but the majority transmit information through their social media accounts, which foreign journalists pick up.

Most foreign journalists reporting on Syria today are doing so from outside the country's borders. Entering the country illegally is far too dangerous, and even those who take the risk run into difficulties finding news outlets to publish their work; many news outlets prohibit accepting freelancers' reports due to the personal risk. Visas to report in government-controlled areas are not impossible to obtain, but after being hacked by the Syrian Electronic Army for my reporting and writing extensively on ISIS, my chances of getting one are slim.

Some foreign journalists still go into Syria, and despite the risks, I tried to go myself at the end of 2015 when Syrian activists started a media campaign to draw attention to the thousands of people living under siege in Madaya, outside Damascus. Civilians have been trapped and starving in Madaya since July 2015, but as a result of the media campaign, by year's end, the city was being covered in the media with unprecedented intensity. Pictures and reports from Syrian journalists and activists of emaciated, undernourished and starved children flooded Twitter and Facebook pages.

The people in Madaya are apparently surrounded and being besieged by Hezbollah, the armed Lebanese group fighting alongside the Syrian regime. Yet when I began trying to get into the city, Hezbollah was telling an entirely different story than was elsewhere reported: There was no siege; people weren't starving; there was food. So unwavering was Hezbollah about this that some of its fighters offered to take me to the outskirts of the town so I could see for myself the available cornucopia of supplies.

I can't go into all the details of why that trip never happened (ironically, I must self-censor), but after several calls and one home visit in Beirut from the FBI, I decided the risk would be too high. Months later, Hezbollah and Syrian regime supporters in Beirut continue to echo their claims, while pictures of emaciated civilians continue to circulate and at least 86 people are known to have died of starvation.

Madaya is a microcosm of the Syrian conflict and raises questions I have pondered since I began covering the war: How could two groups so firmly expound drastically different truths about the situation? And who is right?

A cornerstone of the Syrian regime's public relations campaign since the beginning of the conflict has been to dismiss photographs of violence or the brutal effects of war as opposition or "terrorist" propaganda. Even as I write this, Assad has just told the Associated Press that "if there's really a siege around the city of Aleppo, people would have been dead by now." But the humanitarian workers and activists on the ground send evidence of the siege nearly every day. Assad has an answer for that, too: "If you want to talk about some who allegedly are claiming this, we tell them how could you still be alive? . . . The reality is telling."

Yet the portrayal of reality in Syria is almost always biased. At the start of the war, the majority of people inside Syria were forced to choose a side. Soon after, foreign governments followed suit, voicing support for one cause or another. For the most part, foreign media are still trying to resist this demand to declare allegiance in Syria. But with every story we tell, we risk being labeled either pro-opposition or pro-government: If we publish that Assad is starving his people, we are pro-opposition; if we include that Assad denies these claims, we are enabling a criminal regime. It is meanwhile extremely difficult for us to report undeniable truths from the field.

In response, we have begun to adapt to being sequestered, finding ways to more accurately report on Syria even if we aren't there. During the siege of Aleppo (still ongoing at the time of this writing), dozens of Syrian journalists and activists communicated real-time updates through a massive WhatsApp group, answering foreign journalists' questions and sharing photos and videos. For the most part, though, our coverage is necessarily watered down. It is carefully couched and neutralized just in case it isn't true. It is difficult to call a spade a spade when you haven't seen it yourself.

There are days when we throw up our hands in frustration and feign surrender, lamenting that "everyone is lying to me about Syria!" Still, we can't give up. Everyone may be lying, but the war is real. We may not get visas, and even if we do, our risk assessments for trips to Syria may not be approved. Our attempts to uncover the truth may continue to be met with threats and accusations of bias. As long as there are people in Syria who want to tell their stories, we will try to find a way to make them heard. But for the majority of us, being denied the ability to observe circumstances firsthand means that our necessary circumspection and caution, and our desire to remain unbiased, become a form of censorship, too.

Alessandria Masi is managing editor of Syria Deeply *and Beirut bureau chief of* News Deeply.

2. From Fledgling to Failed

By Jacey Fortin

South Sudanese government soldiers stand in trenches in Malakal in October 2016. The army flew in journalists to show that they retain control of the city, which has been reduced to rubble and almost entirely deserted by civilians.

(AP/Justin Lynch)

J uba, South Sudan—The shooting began around 5:15 on a Friday afternoon.

Dozens of journalists had gathered in the pressroom at the Presidential Palace—a walled compound also known as "J1"—in the capital city. Following a few days of rising tensions, culminating in a checkpoint shoot-out just the night before, the president, Salva Kiir, and the vice president, Riek Machar, former wartime rivals, were expected to hold a news conference calling for peace.

The journalists had been waiting for a couple of hours when they heard gunfire outside. Most of them dropped to the floor. A woman working security by the door fumbled with a gun she didn't seem to know how to operate, making everyone nervous.

After about an hour, the shooting subsided and Kiir and Machar finally appeared, first to urge calm following the gunfire, about which they professed to know little, then to give prepared speeches about the state of the nation.

It was the day before the fifth anniversary of South Sudan's independence.

The journalists waited for hours until it was deemed safe to leave J1. Around midnight, they piled into the beds of pickup trucks and were escorted by soldiers back to a hotel. None were hurt. Some had spotted bloodied corpses on the pavement as they made their way out of the gates.

"The incident at J1," as it has become known in government parlance, marked a new era for South Sudan. The world's youngest country has had a succession of such eras, beginning in 2005, when decades of war against the armed forces of Sudan ended and a fledgling southern government was supposed to be laying the framework for a new state.

Then came 2011, when a landslide referendum created an independent nation. High-ranking officials in the Sudan People's Liberation Army, or SPLA, set themselves to the task of building a nation—a daunting task for a group of war veterans who had made a career of armed struggle.

December 2013 saw the beginning of a civil war that would kill tens of thousands and displace millions, pitting those loyal to President Kiir, a member of the Dinka ethnic group, against those loyal to former Vice President Machar, a member of the Nuer ethnic group. Amid the upheaval, censorship efforts only worsened, with the government often equating criticism with opposition sympathies.

In April 2016, in accordance with a peace deal, Machar moved back to Juba to resume his post as Kiir's deputy so that the two could preside over the formation of a new transitional government.

That arrangement grew increasingly tense. After clashes erupted at J1 in July, they spread across the city, killing hundreds. Machar and his troops were forced out of town. He remains in exile, while skirmishes outside the capital continue, reminiscent of the civil war that was supposed to have ended.

■ ■ ■

With each passing era, the state of press freedom and media censorship has only gotten worse. Even during peacetime, there was a concerted effort to thwart the establishment of a free press in the nascent country: Journalists faced arrests, outlets suffered shutdowns, and media protection laws were ignored. But war has only made things worse, creating an atmosphere of increased militancy and fear. Journalists know that an article deemed to be criticizing the president or his cronies could cost them their freedom or even their lives. Government workers have been known to appear at printing presses to excise newspaper articles deemed offensive. Even the U.N. has made it difficult for journalists to access key information.

Things have never been easy, observed Emmanuel Tombe, deputy director of Bakhita Radio, a community station in Juba. Like so many other local media organizations, Bakhita's first challenge has been simply to stay afloat in a dismal economy. It is a daily struggle even to cover the basics such as staff salaries, studio equipment and generator fuel.

Bakhita is first and foremost a Catholic station, with an emphasis on family-friendly sermons and religious hymns. But it also had three English-language shows dedicated to current events, so it has not been immune to government intimidation, threatened shutdowns and even attacks on staffers in the years since its founding in 2006.

"With the conflict right now, the media is even more threatened," Tombe said in August 2016. Not only did insecurity make it harder to get community funding, it also caused the station to tone down its political reporting, including shutting down "Wake Up Juba," a morning show that sought to engage government leaders in discussions about local problems. The show touched on everything from low-level corruption to political upheavals. In another concession, the station stopped taking outside callers to ensure that no one stirred up controversy on-air.

"The station could be shut down or taken to court; anything could happen," Tombe said. "We also have to worry about the presenter of the program. If the presenter is at risk, his safety can be ensured when he's within the office. But when he's home, what will happen? Nobody knows." For now, lying low strikes Tombe as the best way to protect his staffers and to keep the cash-strapped station afloat.

By mid-July 2016, it had become clear that the government, having pushed Machar's troops out of the city, seemed all the more eager to clamp down on free speech, especially after its soldiers committed a fresh wave of brutal human rights abuses against civilians. That has forced some journalists to self-censor, for fear of provoking a government whose military has never shown respect for media freedoms. Other journalists, both local and foreign, have chosen to leave the country altogether.

One of the most experienced foreign correspondents in South Sudan, freelancer Jason Patinkin, left the country in August 2016. He had just filed a story for The Associated Press documenting a gruesome rape epidemic, mostly committed by SPLA soldiers against Nuer women. "Given the sensitivity of the story I wrote, which was heavily attacked by these pro-government trolls online, whom many believe are on the payroll of the government, I didn't feel safe," he said. "So I left, and I still don't necessarily feel safe going back."

But escape is not an option for everyone. "Of course South Sudanese journalists face far, far greater risks and greater restrictions than foreign journalists," Patinkin said. "The things they put up with for their belief in the truth about South Sudan has my deepest honor."

■ ■ ■

"This is my country. I know people who fought and died for this country," said Hakim George Hakim, a South Sudanese video correspondent for Reuters. "And I believe that the only difference between a journalist and a soldier is that we are fighting with our pen and our opinion, while the soldier has a firearm."

Hakim says that both the government and the opposition are deserving of criticism. But his opinions have gotten him into trouble many times. From what he can tell, the blowback comes not in response to his professional work, but to the views he expresses on his personal Facebook page, which are mostly general posts about how journalists should not be targeted and how the government and the opposition are both failing the people. His professional work—mostly videography for a newswire—cannot serve as a platform for his opinions, but he is dedicated to vocalizing his thoughts on social media to push for peace in South Sudan.

In 2016, someone broke into Hakim's parked car and took only an envelope of personal documents. He has been trailed by government vehicles more than once. He has been warned that his name had been placed on a no-fly list at Juba International Airport. He has received dozens of anonymous phone calls asking him to take down certain Facebook posts.

Some of those calls threatened violence. "Somebody would call me and say, 'Do you want your family to cry soon? About losing you?'" he said.

Not all media workers who lost their lives in 2016 were targeted for their work. Kamula Duro, a cameraman working for President Kiir himself, died of gunshot wounds during the clashes in July, with no suggestion that he was intentionally targeted.

Shortly thereafter, a journalist working for the international organization Internews was gunned down while sheltering in a hotel compound on the outskirts of Juba. John Gatluak had been working for Internews for four years and was by all accounts a thoughtful, professional and notably dedicated journalist. The scarification on his forehead identified him clearly as a member of the Nuer ethnic group, and Internews believes it was this alone—not Gatluak's work—that singled him out for a summary execution on July 11, 2016.

Still, there is no question that journalists' work has put them at risk. At a press conference in August 2015, President Kiir made a statement that has lived in infamy ever since. "The freedom of press does not mean that you work against your country," he said. "And if anybody among them does not know that this country has killed people, we will demonstrate it one day on them."

Four days later, the newspaper journalist Peter Moi was shot dead by unknown assailants as he walked home from work. And in December 2015, newspaper editor Joseph Afandi was arrested and detained for nearly two months, possibly in connection with an article criticizing the SPLA. In March 2016, just weeks after his release, Afandi was abducted, severely beaten and dumped near a cemetery in the capital.

"They try to terrorize you and scare you," Hakim said. "We have many examples in South Sudan. When somebody doesn't like what some journalist did, his boys, or his gang, can execute the plan of eliminating that journalist. It happens a lot."

Asked about these incidents, the government simply denies that any problems exist. "There is no harassment," said Information Minister Michael Makuei. "These stories about intimidation have been concocted. Otherwise, they should have reported it to us at the ministry."

But media workers here know that the information ministry is not a safe space. Foreign and local journalists alike are sometimes summoned there to be berated—at length—by ministry officials and intelligence agents who accuse them of producing stories that are biased against the government.

■ ■ ■

Sometimes, the summons comes not from the information ministry but from the security and intelligence agency—and that, journalists know, is a sign of trouble.

It happened to Alfred Taban, who is perhaps South Sudan's most celebrated and well-known journalist. For decades, he worked in the restrictive media environment of Khartoum, Sudan. But when his country first achieved independence in 2011, Taban moved south to become the founder and editor-in-chief of the *Juba Monitor*, which is now South Sudan's most prominent English-language daily newspaper.

In all this time, Taban has never been afraid to write articles critical of the government. But things took a turn when, after the clashes, he wrote an opinion piece calling for both Kiir and Machar to step down. On July 16, 2016, the editor was called to the intelligence agency and then put behind bars. He would not be released on bail until two weeks later.

"[Officials] used to call me to their offices and complain about my articles, and somehow we would reach an understanding," he said, sitting in his office behind a desk stacked high with old newspapers. "But this time, without any warning, they just threw me inside. So this was really a clear sign they were not interested in dialogue."

Despite suffering medical problems, including diabetes, high blood pressure and a malarial infection, Taban was initially refused admission to a hospital. That changed when he requested a different doctor, one who was not in league with the security officials. He was released from jail shortly thereafter.

Upon returning to the office, he quickly discovered that the government had other ways to censor his work; plainclothes security agents were going to the private printing press where *Juba Monitor* is produced and demanding certain articles be cut.

He pointed to the August 4, 2016, edition of the paper, where a big blank spot took up nearly half the page. That was supposed to be a news report about Pagan Amum, an SPLA veteran now critical of the government, who had called for a team of technocrats to take over the country's administration. But the security agents had removed the article and asked the printers to place an advertisement there to fill the space.

Taban intervened by removing the ad, knowing that blank spaces can speak volumes. "The purpose is to let the people realize that there is very serious censorship," he said.

Taban says South Sudan's media environment has never been worse. But one good thing came from his time in detention: He got the rare chance to speak, face to face, with George Livio.

Livio had been working as a radio journalist employed by the U.N. Mission in South Sudan, or UNMISS, when he was arrested in the western town of Wau on August 22, 2014. He has been detained for more than two years with no formal charges filed against him. (CPJ has never been able to determine a link between his imprisonment and his journalistic work and has not included him on its annual prison census.)

An official with the intelligence agency, Ramadan Chadar, said in August 2016 that he had never heard of Livio's case. He said Oliver Modi, the head of the Union of Journalists in South Sudan—a nominally independent media organization—might have more information. Modi knew of the case but said that it was "a security issue" in the hands of the intelligence agencies.

In this way, both men—each referring the problem to the other's organization, even as the two sat right next to each other—wiped their hands clean of the issue.

Taban said that Livio was sharing a small cell with three other inmates in a compound where dozens of men had access to a single toilet and were fed once a day. It was almost always the same dish: beans with too much salt, Taban said. Livio also told Taban that UNMISS had not been allowed to visit Livio for months.

"The treatment of these people was what disturbed me. I was not so much thinking about myself; I was thinking about them. Because the accusations against them are ridiculous," Taban said, adding that most had been accused of working with the opposition.

■ ■ ■

Even Livio's own former employer has remained quiet. UNMISS has not once publicly called for his release, and officials, when pressed, always insist that they are working on it behind the scenes. "We are raising the issue of [his] release over and over again with the relevant authorities," said UNMISS head Ellen Margrethe Løj in May 2016.

To date, that method has failed Livio, and many journalists here aren't surprised. UNMISS has a strained relationship with the media in South Sudan, having shown reluctance to relay essential information or even to allow journalists access to its displacement camps across the country.

Freelance journalist Justin Lynch took a U.N. flight to visit one such camp, in the northern city of Malakal, in February 2016. He happened to touch down in the middle of a vicious attack. Men wearing

SPLA uniforms had stormed the camp, killed civilians and burned down tents. When all was said and done, at least 25 people had lost their lives.

It was clear that the U.N. peacekeepers had utterly failed to protect the displaced, only stepping in when it was far too late.

Almost immediately after Lynch landed, officials at the UNMISS Public Information Office ordered him to leave, but other U.N. staffers encouraged him to stay. "On the night of the 17th, the U.N. made a statement saying the attack was done by 'armed youth,'" he said. "And I think a lot of people at the U.N. Mission in Malakal were really angry, because we knew it was the SPLA, and we knew that the peacekeepers had fled."

With help from these sympathetic staffers, Lynch repeatedly dodged U.N. officials who were trying to track him down and put him on an airplane.

"Whenever you block access like that, it's conducive to a closed environment where these kinds of problems can fester," Lynch said. He stayed at the camp for five days and eventually published a series of reports—many of which were published by the *Daily Beast*—that challenged UNMISS's version of events and exposed the peacekeepers' failures. In December 2016, he was deported from South Sudan.

Patinkin agrees that in a country where censorship is already rife, the United Nations doesn't make things any easier. He said the situation has gotten worse with time, citing a host of obstacles including U.N. staffers' refusals to report clashes, restrictions on access to the camps and arbitrary price hikes for U.N. flights.

"I have even been yelled at by UNMISS spokespersons," he added. "I mean, the level of unprofessionalism from the UNMISS PIO has at times been shocking."

■ ■ ■

Incidents like these only add to an atmosphere of censorship in this war-torn country. And no matter where the censorship comes from, it is not only journalists who suffer—it is the entire population, which came together with so much hope when South Sudan became a nation in 2011. When local outlets are afraid to voice criticism, the U.N.

restricts access, newspapers are subject to the whims of security officials and talented journalists see no option but to leave, there is a gaping void of information that the government is keen to fill with its own propaganda.

The journalists here do what they can, but the trauma of reporting in a country like this wears them thin. For some, the fatigue is palpable. The foreigners come and go, leaving the country when it becomes too difficult or too dangerous. The locals flee when they are able, though sometimes they have nowhere to run to.

In the view of video journalist Hakim George Hakim, someone has to stay to fight for South Sudan's great potential. Hakim believes that someday, generations from now, a peaceful country will look back on these early years with a sense of relief that the worst is over.

"Now the country has reached a level where the government knows that the people know that this is a failed state," he said. "And they don't want anybody to talk about that. So if you try to criticize the government's performance, you're going to get some problems."

But he says he'll keep trying anyway, no matter what.

Jacey Fortin is a freelance journalist who reports from Ethiopia and South Sudan.

3. A Loyal Press

By Ursula Lindsey

A protest against the jailing of photojournalist Mahmoud Abou Zeid, known as Shawkan, in front of the Journalists' Syndicate in Cairo on July 12, 2014. Egypt has sought to silence its critics in recent years.

(AP/Amr Nabil)

W hen President Abdel Fattah el-Sisi took office in Egypt in 2014, after leading the army's ouster of Islamist President Mohamed Morsi, he promised to restore peace and prosperity through strong leadership.

But in the years since, Sisi's idea of strength has been to silence those who disagree with him and to treat criticism or the documentation of abuses as a threat to national security. His government has developed unprecedented new strategies to limit free speech, which include exploiting and encouraging polarization within the media—turning journalists against one another—and undermining the public's trust in the media, in concert with familiar censorship tactics, such as withholding advertising from media outlets to force them to self-censor.

Sisi has presided over a foundering economy, a growing insurgency in the Sinai Peninsula and a series of erratic, unaccountable policy decisions and has responded to the inevitable questions and complaints of Egyptian citizens and the media with further repression. While tens of thousands of Egyptians serve time as political prisoners, Sisi's security services have kidnapped, tortured and detained citizens in secret locations, sometimes forcing them to confess to fabricated crimes.

Journalists have been on the front line of the struggle to defend crumbling freedoms and the rule of law, and Egyptian authorities are using any means at their disposal to silence, intimidate and punish reporters who do not reproduce official propaganda. Journalists who report on human rights abuses, who cover protests or who report criticism of government policies are treated as disloyal enemies and targeted for retribution.

That retribution takes many forms, from using favored media to smear and attack "disloyal" journalists to withholding advertising revenue from media outlets that have been critical of the government or have simply reported on its failures. Other tactics represent an unprecedented escalation of older means of repression, such as imprisoning, sentencing to death, deporting or otherwise harassing journalists. In its determination to prevent the kinds of mass mobilizations that took place during the Arab Spring, the Sisi government will not tolerate any dissent and has shown deep suspicions of regional media outlets it sees as destabilizing influences.

"The mainstream media is still very faithful to the president and very propagandistic," said Shahira Amin, a journalist who resigned from state TV during the uprising against former President Hosni Mubarak. Due to her own critical reporting, Amin said she is no longer allowed to work in television in Egypt.

In 2016, Amin said, "Critical voices started to emerge, reflecting growing disappointment" in Sisi, who she contends "hasn't delivered the security and stability he promised." Such criticism is unacceptable to a president who has admonished the Egyptian public, saying: "Listen only to me." The result is a continuous spiral of instability, dissent and further repression. "The criticism has increased," Amin said. "But also they're trying to crack down even harder."

Despite the censorship and repression, the country's lively independent media has struggled on, in many cases moving to online platforms that are more difficult to control, though not immune to acts of retribution. A prison census released by the Committee to Protect Journalists on December 1, 2016, found that Egyptian authorities were holding at least 25 journalists behind bars due to their reporting—the highest in the country since CPJ began recording data on imprisoned journalists in 1990. The threat of imprisonment is part of an atmosphere of relentless intimidation in which authorities issue gag orders on sensitive topics and pressure media outlets to censor critical reports. Entire news outlets, such as Al-Jazeera and the Turkish Anadolu Agency, have been banned from operating or forced to close their offices, according to CPJ research.

In the spring of 2016, three journalists were sentenced to death in absentia, and others were deported without any legal justification, held in preventive detention beyond the legal limit of two years, or charged with crimes such as terrorism, vandalism, murder, or publishing false news. The Sisi government also targeted the Journalists' Syndicate, entering its premises to arrest two reporters and bringing charges against the group's leaders after they spoke out in solidarity with their detained colleagues.

■ ■ ■

According to CPJ research, Egypt has become one of the worst jailers of journalists in the world, behind only Turkey and China in 2016.

Journalists are frequently arrested by security forces in nighttime raids on their homes, and some have faced patently fabricated charges, been tortured in custody or seen their families harassed. Journalists have been targeted simply for reporting on protests and human rights abuses, such as the deadly dispersal of a sit-in at the Rabaa El Adawiya square in Cairo in August 2013—a massacre in which at least 600 supporters of deposed President Morsi were killed by security forces, according to published reports and figures kept by Egypt's Ministry of Health.

In April 2015, CPJ documented three journalists sentenced to life in prison. Those and other journalists were accused of "fabricating pictures and scenes that imply fatalities and injuries among demonstrators, preparing statements in foreign languages and publishing all of this outside Egypt to imply that security forces used excessive force and violated human rights," according to the Alkarama human rights non-governmental organization.

Another journalist who was imprisoned for documenting what happened at Rabaa is news photographer Mahmoud Abou Zeid, known as Shawkan, who was arrested on August 14, 2013, while photographing the security operation on the square for the agency Demotix. Shawkan, who addressed an Egyptian court for the first time in May 2016, told the judge, "I am in jail for doing my job."

The emaciated 27-year-old had by then been in detention for more than 1,000 days, a violation of Article 143 of the Code of Criminal Procedures, which calls for the immediate release of any detainee held in pretrial detention for more than two years without being sentenced. "We ask for his release at each session," lawyer Taher Abu Nasr said in July 2016, "but the court does not respond."

"There is no evidence against him. He shouldn't have spent one day in jail," Shawkan's brother, Mohamed Abou Zeid, said in a telephone interview in July 2016.

Alongside 738 other defendants, including the Supreme Guide of the Muslim Brotherhood, Shawkan went on trial in December 2015, charged with illegal protesting, the use of force, illegal arms possession, vandalism with "a terrorist intent," belonging to a banned group (the Brotherhood), attacking police forces and murder—charges that carry a potential death penalty, according to Shawkan's lawyer and Amnesty International reports.

In a March 2015 letter from prison posted on Amnesty International's website, Shawkan said he has been beaten during his detention and denied access to medical treatment for his injuries. "I share a cell that measures three by four meters with 12 political prisoners," he wrote. "We have no access to sun or fresh air for days or weeks at a time. My detention has been renewed ever since my arrest for 600 days. I have not been charged with any crime. I have been imprisoned without any investigation into the fabricated charges I am facing. I am a photojournalist, not a criminal. My indefinite detention is psychologically unbearable. Not even animals would survive in these conditions."

In a December 2015 letter, Shawkan wrote: "Of course after more than 850 days in the black hole without fairness and justice, I am lost in limbo. Just because I was doing my job as a photographer. I am in jail without even knowing why am I here? I'm sorry to tell you that 'I became a person full of hopelessness.'"

That hopelessness is shared by his family. "He is in a bad psychological and physical state," said his brother, who fears that the authorities, having kept Shawkan in jail for more than two years before bringing charges, will now drag out the trial for many more years. "The lawyer can't do anything, civil society can't do anything, nobody can do anything—he will just die," Mohamed Abou Zeid said.

Around the time Shawkan was speaking in his own defense in court for the first time, three journalists received death sentences in a separate case. Ibrahim Helal, the former news director at Al-Jazeera Arabic; Alaa Sablan, a reporter at Al-Jazeera; and Asmaa Al-Khatib, a news editor at Rassd News Network, were accused, alongside former President Morsi and seven others, of attempting to share state secrets with Qatar. In May 2016, the three journalists were sentenced to death in absentia.

Al-Jazeera Arabic supported the uprising against former President Mubarak and, in the years after, provided a platform and sympathetic coverage to the Muslim Brotherhood. Qatar, the wealthy emirate where the network is based, was widely viewed as backing the Islamist group.

Hours after the military detained Morsi, soldiers stormed Al-Jazeera Arabic's offices in Cairo, forcing the channel to go off the air. Following its fall from power, the Brotherhood was classified as a terrorist group, and Qatar and Al-Jazeera were accused of plotting alongside the organization to destabilize and take over the country. In an infamous case, 10 Al-Jazeera reporters were convicted of aiding a terrorist organization. Seven were tried in absentia; among those held in Egypt, one was deported and two who remained were granted presidential pardons after an international solidarity campaign and years of lobbying on their behalf.

Relations between Egypt and Qatar have remained deeply strained. In February 2015, after Qatar questioned Egypt's military operations in Libya, Egyptian officials accused Qatar of "backing terrorism," and the state-owned *Al Ahram* newspaper ran a headline calling Qatar (alongside Turkey and the United States) part of "The Triangle of the Forces of Evil [that] Spreads Chaos and Destruction."

Ibrahim Helal, the Al-Jazeera news director tried in absentia, believes some in the Egyptian media and government find it easier to blame Qatar and Al-Jazeera for supposed plots than to face the country's many problems.

"They live in this illusion of enemies fighting the country," Helal said, "instead of facing the reality that the country is failing because of lack of democracy and human rights." Helal, who lives in exile in Doha, added, "If it was a democratic country I would try to go back to defend myself." But, he said, "you know how many people are dying in custody in Egypt today."

■ ■ ■

Among the few institutions that have continued to speak out on behalf of imprisoned or otherwise targeted reporters is the Journalists' Syndicate, which, because it has offered refuge and solidarity to journalists, has become a target itself. The government's animosity toward the organization became clear after an incident involving two islands in the Red Sea that were ceded by Egypt to Saudi Arabia in the spring of 2016.

The unexpected announcement regarding the ceding of the islands triggered a wave of nationalist indignation in Egypt, and growing frustration with Sisi culminated in the first significant public protest since the beginning of his term, on April 15, 2016. Columnists and TV presenters also engaged in unprecedented criticism of the president and his government.

The authorities reacted swiftly, arresting hundreds of the protesters, many of whom were later sentenced to three- to five-year jail terms. The government also punished journalists who covered the demonstrations and placed a gag order on the island transfer and the protests surrounding it. It has resorted to such media blackouts with increasing frequency on topics ranging from the murder of Italian student Giulio Regeni to military operations in the Sinai.

Editor Amr Badr and reporter Mahmoud al-Sakka, both of the news website *Yanair*, were charged with spreading false news, inciting the public and plotting to overthrow the government because of their coverage of the island transfer and the protests. After their homes were raided by police, the two journalists sought refuge inside the Journalists' Syndicate offices in central Cairo, planning to camp out there and publicize their plight.

The syndicate has long been a "safe zone" for journalists and for freedom of speech, hosting press conferences on sensitive topics and gatherings, including protests, on its front steps. The police have frequently blocked off the surrounding streets and cordoned off the area but refrained from entering the building, which under Egyptian law requires an order from the public prosecutor and the presence of the syndicate head. In keeping with Sisi's increasingly drastic measures against the media, breaking with precedent and the law, police raided the building and arrested Badr and al-Sakka. Eyewitnesses said dozens of national security officers forced their way past the syndicate's security guards. "This is the first time that this has happened in Egypt's history," Khaled El-Balshy, editor of the website *Albedaiah* and head of the syndicate's Freedom Committee, said.

The security forces' actions led to a sit-in and a statement issued by journalists calling for the resignation of the minister of interior and the release of all jailed journalists. The ministry's response was that only four officers had entered the syndicate offices and that Badr and Sakka had willingly turned themselves over to their custody (the authorities also claimed they had an order from the public prosecutor, but others say agents did not produce one at the time). Emails from the ministry

that included directions on how to handle the crisis were later acciden-
tally leaked, which suggested that security experts be sent to "friendly"
TV talk shows to promote the ministry's version of events. One email
argued that the ministry "cannot retreat from its position now, because
to retreat would mean a mistake had been made, and if there was one,
who would be responsible and who would be held accountable?"

At first, almost all Egyptian media outlets—including state-owned
ones—expressed indignation over the police raid. But within days, many
outlets began distancing themselves from the syndicate and blaming its
leadership for allegedly politicizing and escalating the conflict. Some
commentators said the syndicate was overstepping its bounds and being
manipulated by the Muslim Brotherhood. For offering refuge to their
colleagues and for publicizing the police's actions, El-Balshy, as well as
syndicate head Yehia al-Kalash, and union secretary-general Gamal
Abdel-Reheem were charged with harboring wanted fugitives and
spreading false news that destabilizes and incites public opinion.

El-Balshy believed that the prosecution against him and his colleagues was meant to weaken the syndicate, which had expressed res-
ervations over a proposed new press law, had lobbied on behalf of
imprisoned journalists like Shawkan and had denounced dawn raids,
punitive detentions and forced disappearances of reporters.

"The point is to put pressure on the syndicate, to prevent it from
playing its role and defending its members," El-Balshy said.

Jail terms and death sentences are the worst threats against reporters, though Egyptian journalists trying to report critically and independently face other state-sponsored intimidation as well, including being
monitored, threatened or targeted with smear campaigns. Deportation
and travel bans have also become increasingly common. Local reporters may discover at the airport that they have been banned from travel,
while foreign journalists are more likely to be detained as they enter
the country or to be unexpectedly expelled.

On June 27, 2016, TV host Liliane Daoud was arrested at her
home in Cairo. Daoud, who is British-Lebanese, was the presenter of
the Egyptian talk show "The Full Picture" on ONtv, one of the few
remaining platforms in Egyptian media on which one could hear critical discussions of government officials and policies. Daoud's contract
with ONtv had been terminated earlier that day.

The police who entered her house and ordered her to leave with them immediately said their orders had come directly from the Interior Ministry and from "the president's office," Daoud afterward told reporters. She was not charged with any crime. As the mother of an Egyptian child (Daoud's ex-husband is Egyptian), she has a legal right to reside in Egypt, but she told *The New York Times* she had been threatened with deportation several times in the previous year, and the authorities had declined to renew her residency, citing security concerns. Members of her production team were also threatened with arrest, she said.

An unnamed security official told The Associated Press on June 28, 2016, that Daoud had crossed "red lines" in her program, in which she had dedicated episodes to jailed activists, prison conditions and forced disappearances.

"Despite the difficult circumstances we've been working under for the last five years," Daoud told Misr Live News, "we never expected the ceiling of freedom to fall as low as it has now."

Lamis El Hadidi, a TV presenter who has been a vocal supporter of both former President Mubarak and President Sisi, said on the air that when considering Daoud's case and other instances of journalist intimidation, "We are very anxious. Are these signs? Are they signals? Are we supposed to stop talking? To just keep quiet?"

■ ■ ■

Given the vocal and widespread public support for the army and for Sisi after the ousting of the Muslim Brotherhood in 2013, many observers find it remarkable how much repression has been unleashed against reporters and how hard pro-government interests have worked to further consolidate and monopolize the media field.

The channel for which Daoud formerly worked had recently been sold by businessman Naguib Sawiris to steel tycoon Ahmed Abu Hashima, who is a Sisi supporter and a major donor to his Long Live Egypt fund. When Sisi visited New York City in September 2015, Hashima was reportedly the main financier of a pro-Egypt campaign that featured ads in *The Wall Street Journal* and billboards in Times Square. Hashima also has a majority stake in *Al Youm Al Sabaa* newspaper and is said to be planning other media buys, according to numerous media reports.

Egypt is a highly concentrated media market, and as the independent news site *Mada Masr* has documented, the businessmen who own the country's top eight private TV channels enjoy cordial relations with the government. The majority are major donors to the Long Live Egypt fund.

The businessmen know it is in their interest to express support for and loyalty to Sisi. In November 2015, a heavily armed, masked police unit dragged Salah Diab, the owner of *Al Masry Al Youm* newspaper, from his bed and arrested him on charges of possessing unlicensed firearms. Pictures of Diab in handcuffs were taken by a photographer from *Al Youm Al Sabaa*, the tabloid that Hashima owns and that regularly gets scoops based on security tips.

Observers wondered if the raid was caused by *Al Masry Al Youm*'s coverage or some offending remark Diab had made about Sisi. The newspaper tycoon lent credence to the second conjecture when he published a column upon his release, worrying that something had damaged his relationship with the president—"a word of mine"—and insisting that he had not meant to criticize and that he loved the president "like millions of loyal Egyptians."

The majority of the country's most-respected columnists and TV hosts, who headlined hard-hitting political talk shows in the years following the 2011 uprisings, have quit or had their columns and programs canceled in recent years. And the security services have gone beyond blacklisting certain reporters and guests: They now routinely pressure media owners and leak information—including recordings of personal phone calls—in their targeting of activists and journalists.

According to an investigative report by activist and journalist Hossam Bahgat, officers from Egypt's General Intelligence Directorate have written pseudonymous columns in the Egyptian media as well as run a media front company that acquired a news website and produced a TV show. Bahgat has since been detained and questioned over his reporting on the army and now faces trial on charges related to the Egyptian Initiative for Personal Rights, the NGO he founded.

State media and privately owned media run by businessmen eager to curry favor with the presidency, or aligned with the security services, are often the first to attack other outlets and reporters if they publish critical stories. "The smear campaigns are worse than ever," Shahira Amin said. "If you're a government critic, you're accused of being a spy and a traitor." Amin has been accused by Egyptian media outlets close to the government of promoting homosexuality, being an atheist and being "a friend of the Jews." She was also accused, she says, "of being in a shadow government formed in Berlin to topple President el-Sisi."

When Amin confronted the editor of a state-owned magazine that published some of these rumors, she says he told her: "Well, if you're not with us, you're against the state. In war times there is no in-between."

After a meeting with EU officials to discuss media freedoms in Egypt, in which Amin noted the repression reporters face, a colleague took her to court, accusing her of spreading false news, tarnishing Egypt's image abroad and damaging its interests. (Amin was eventually acquitted.)

These episodes illustrate how Egypt's media have been intimidated, silenced, infiltrated, co-opted and incited to attack fellow journalists. By relentlessly questioning journalists' patriotism and amalgamating their actions to terrorism and espionage, the authorities have also broken down public trust in them.

"The past three years of intense propaganda have turned every last member of the Egyptian population, you feel, against journalists," said Nour Youssef, a reporter who has worked with the AP and *The New York Times*. "You can feel it with every story—people genuinely believe you are a spy, are scared to speak, are aggressive. It's increasingly hard to talk to normal people, not just government officials."

Ursula Lindsey *writes about education, culture, media and politics in the Arab world.*

4. What Is the Worst-Case Scenario?

By Alan Huffman

A member of the crowd holds up a copy of the U.S. Constitution at a campaign rally for Donald Trump in Rhode Island in April 2016.

(Reuters/Brian Snyder)

The word *unprecedented* is often used to describe Donald Trump's antipathy toward the American media, as it is of many of his other approaches to governance.

Yet for veteran U.S. journalist Bill Minor, Trump's rhetoric and the threat it poses to the media have a hauntingly familiar ring. Minor, who covered the civil rights movement in Mississippi in the 1950s and 1960s for the New Orleans *Times-Picayune*, recalls a time when journalists faced harassment from government officials, courts, police and angry crowds, most of whom had little interest in First Amendment protections.

Journalists in Mississippi during the era who refused to toe the line were often put under surveillance or jailed, and hostile paralegal groups such as the Ku Klux Klan and the White Citizens, Councils operated with something close to impunity. Reporters and photographers were frequently threatened with violence, and their publishers faced lawsuits and advertising boycotts, the latter of which drove some outlets out of business.

"It was like we were in a foreign country," Minor recalled recently from his home in Jackson, Mississippi, where he still works as a newspaper columnist at 94.

Though Minor's newspaper's location across the state line insulated him to some degree from local financial pressures, he was spied on and received death threats and, while covering an effort to desegregate the bus station in the city of McComb, Mississippi, witnessed a group of men assaulting a *Life* magazine photographer and a *Time* magazine reporter who were walking with him "right there on Main Street."

Such violence against the media occurred across the South, including at the University of Mississippi in 1962, where a French reporter was shot and killed during a riot over the school's integration. No one was ever charged in that crime. Minor recalled that the offices of *The Lexington Advertiser*—one of the few newspapers in Mississippi that reported on police brutality against black residents—were bombed, and its owner, Hazel Brannon Smith, was bankrupted by financial losses incurred as a result of an advertising boycott and the expense of defending herself against a series of libel suits, including one filed by the local sheriff.

Given such challenges to journalists during the civil rights era, Minor is deeply concerned by what he sees as "the rebirth of an old animosity against the press," particularly given its potentially far broader scope today. He said journalists cannot afford to be complacent about the potential for crowd violence, government surveillance, expanding libel lawsuits and Trump's open disregard for traditional First Amendment protections.

U.S. journalists typically look to constitutional protections from such attacks; yet, the entire legal structure that protects them and makes the U.S. distinct from the rest of the world emerged only in the last half century. In the tense environment of Mississippi during the civil rights era, "the First Amendment didn't matter," Minor said.

■ ■ ■

Blaming the messenger is a long-standing practice in authoritarian states around the world, which many U.S.-based journalist advocacy organizations, including the Committee to Protect Journalists, have been instrumental in bringing to light.

Yet Trump has taken anti-media hostility to a level that was previously unseen on a national scale in the U.S., which has long been a beacon of hope for the free press, largely due to its constitutional protections. With Trump in the White House, the U.S. media itself seems far less secure, CNN correspondent Christiane Amanpour noted during CPJ's annual awards event in November 2016. "I never in a million years thought I would be up here on stage appealing for the freedom and safety of American journalists at home," Amanpour said during her speech accepting CPJ's Burton Benjamin Memorial Award, which is adapted elsewhere in this book.

The longstanding assumption has been that the First Amendment grants U.S. journalists immunity from the sorts of attacks that their more vulnerable colleagues elsewhere suffer. Yet those protections are contingent upon the support for a free media of both the government and the public.

Public animosity toward the U.S. press has been building for years, as illustrated by derisive comments about the "lamestream media" by 2008 vice presidential candidate Sarah Palin. Such criticism includes charges of bias, sensationalism and failure to challenge falsehoods or distortions. There is evidence to support those criticisms against certain media outlets, though in many cases the charges are levied indiscriminately and without basis in fact.

Social media has further undermined media trust through echo-chamber attacks and the posting of biased or fake news reports, to the point that many Americans consider even independent fact-checking organizations suspect. Some local, state and federal government agencies have meanwhile used bureaucratic hurdles, delays and exorbitant fees to make it harder for enterprising journalists to access public records.

The question is how far the backlash against the free press in the U.S. will go.

In their book *The Race Beat*, journalists Gene Roberts and Hank Klibanoff noted the degree to which press freedom was restricted throughout the worst-case scenario of the American South during the civil rights era. In addition to the kinds of threats Minor described, they wrote of media blackouts, restricted access to public officials and records, and the dissemination of fake news by civil rights opponents. Mississippi's Sovereignty Commission, a now-defunct state agency created to preserve segregation and to monitor opponents and journalists, once paid a black newspaper to plant a fake story that was then picked up by wire services and reported as fact, according to Roberts and Klibanoff.

Minor—on whom the Sovereignty Commission spied, according to records that have since been unsealed—recalled that most of the state's media outlets acquiesced to the powers-that-be, self-censored or reported with a clear segregationist bias. The few that reported objectively faced sure reprisals.

White supremacist organizations also supported Trump during the 2016 presidential campaign, and he cultivated media suspicion and animosity at his rallies, where he corralled and frequently ridiculed journalists whom he described as "disgusting" and "the lowest form of humanity." Crowds at those rallies frequently booed journalists, and in a particularly disturbing image that was widely circulated on social media (and appears on the cover of this book), a supporter wears a T-shirt emblazoned with the words: "Rope. Tree. Journalist. SOME

ASSEMBLY REQUIRED," bringing to mind the notorious lynchings of the civil rights period.

As a candidate, Trump also banished journalists that he perceived as unfriendly, at times denying access to reporters for *Politico*, *BuzzFeed*, *The Huffington Post* and *The Washington Post*. And he vowed to revisit libel laws to make it easier to sue reporters and media outlets, despite the fact that such laws are established and generally enjoy nonpartisan support, and any effort to change them would require the support of Congress and/or the Supreme Court.

Under the Supreme Court's 1964 decision in *New York Times* v. *Sullivan*, which grew from a civil rights–era libel case in Alabama and set the precedent for press freedom in the U.S., public officials who sue media organizations or individual reporters for damages must prove actual malice. During the period that the Supreme Court was hearing the case, *The New York Times* was already fighting six libel suits totaling more than $6 million, and the CBS television network was being sued over its coverage of civil rights crimes in Birmingham, Alabama. Libel lawsuits were then frequently used in the South to try to suppress news coverage, and prior to the higher court ruling, the plaintiffs usually won their cases on the local and state levels.

The media protection that was granted in *New York Times* v. *Sullivan* contrasts with media treatment in countries with less stringent libel laws, such as in India and Brazil, where CPJ has found that journalists are often burdened with hefty fines and legal fees that can have a chilling effect on the flow of information. Notably, any effort to weaken legal libel protections for the media in the U.S. could open social media—Trump's preferred medium—to such suits as well. It is not yet known how Trump's influence on the Supreme Court and on lower federal courts could affect future rulings, or whether local and state courts will follow a similar tack. Trump has specifically threatened to sue *The New York Times* for reporting on his tax returns and on allegations by women that they had been groped and kissed by him without their consent, and to file an antitrust lawsuit against *The Washington Post* owner and Amazon CEO Jeff Bezos. As evidence to the fear such litigious threats instill, *The New York Times* reported in October 2016 that the American Bar Association had decided not to release a report it had commissioned which found that Trump was a "libel bully" bent on punishing or silencing his critics, due to "the risk of the A.B.A. being sued by Mr. Trump."

Like so much of his anti-media rhetoric, Trump's litigation threat taps into a trend.

"Juries have never been the media's best friend . . . but I think we are seeing a trend against the press lately," Sonja R. West, a First Amendment expert at the University of Georgia Law School, told *The Washington Post* on November 5, 2016. "The courts and the public seem to be becoming less likely to give the press the benefit of the doubt and more interested in protecting individuals from what they view as the powerful and sensationalistic media."

The *Post* reported that "mistrust of the media has been growing for decades, according to public surveys." In 2015, "the percentage of people saying they have 'a great deal' or 'a fair amount' of trust in the news media's accuracy and reliability tied its all-time low in a Gallup survey," according to the article.

The *Columbia Journalism Review* reported on October 25, 2016, that a North Carolina jury had awarded nearly $6 million in libel verdicts against *The Raleigh News & Observer* and one of its reporters, which *CJR* said "seems to provide more evidence that the growing unpopularity of media may translate into less-sympathetic jury pools when news organizations face lawsuits." The case also raised concerns among journalists about the security of their communications with sources and editors should they be called to testify, according to *CJR*.

Because Trump sometimes makes provocative statements that he later contradicts or even denies having said, many in the media initially expressed hope that he would soften his stance after being elected president, but so far that has not been the case. He has limited media access to his activities, refusing to allow the traditional pool of reporters, photographers and TV crews to accompany him on trips, and he remains the only president to speak out against the protections of the First Amendment. Journalists and media watchers found cold comfort in his cryptic response when asked during a post-election *New York Times* editorial meeting about his commitment to the First Amendment, and he said, "I think you'll be happy."

All of which raises questions about the long-term security of press freedom in the U.S. and how its potential erosion could affect the media elsewhere in the world.

In an open letter to "Friends in American Journalism" published in the November 22, 2016, *CJR,* Human Rights Watch deputy director for media, Nic Dawes, wrote that the perils of a decline in press freedom in the U.S. under Trump would have dire consequences for everyone.

"Ordinarily, it is you who offer the rest of the world advice about press freedom, and the accountability architecture of democratic societies, so I understand that it may be strange to hear it coming back at you, but this will not be the last inversion that the election of Donald Trump delivers," Dawes wrote. Among the potential consequences, according to Dawes, is a decline of the global standard for press freedom. "For all its real and urgent problems," he wrote, "US journalism is still the City on a Hill. The fading of its light will be disastrous not just for Americans, but for all of us."

Historically, U.S. journalists have not felt the need to band together to protect their profession, largely because of those First Amendment protections, Dawes noted. The U.S. Constitution, he wrote, "offers stronger protections than just about any comparable legal framework." But as Minor pointed out, there have been times when the First Amendment provided little protection on the ground because it was disregarded by rogue state governments. When that happened, the only recourse was the federal government, and particularly, federal courts.

The First Amendment to the Constitution is a legal framework whose interpretation has evolved in the last half century as a result of federal court rulings. Before the Supreme Court's media-supportive rulings, journalists in the U.S.—like their counterparts in other countries—had to fight for their right to report the news. Without those legal protections, they would be equally vulnerable.

The First Amendment, which protects freedom of speech, the press and religion and the right to public assembly and to petition the government for redress of grievances, was literally a revolutionary idea when it was adopted in 1791 and included in the Bill of Rights. During the American Revolution, in 1776, the Virginia colonial legislature had passed a sort of precursor titled a Declaration of Rights that included this sentence: "The freedom of the press is one of the greatest bulwarks of liberty, and can never be restrained but by despotic Governments." Variations of the declaration were adopted by other colonial legislatures, and in the two and a half centuries since, the First Amendment itself has enjoyed rare nonpartisan support.

In his *CJR* article, Dawes, a former editor at India's *Hindustan Times* and at South Africa's *Mail & Guardian*, wrote that in addition to legal protection, journalists in the U.S. have long enjoyed other benefits denied to many of their international peers. Journalists in the U.S., he wrote, generally have stronger financial backing, which, though it is uneven and less secure than it once was, is "orders of magnitude more plentiful than what your counterparts elsewhere have to call upon. You also have reserves of talent, creativity, and commitment far larger than you are given credit for by your critics, and right now by angry, bewildered, and wounded friends."

"But," Dawes added, "one thing you don't have is experience of what to do when things start to get genuinely bad." For example, he wrote, "when Donald Trump ditched his press pool twice within days of being elected, and launched a series of Twitter attacks on the *New York Times*, a lot of you sounded surprised." In fact, he wrote, Trump wasn't bluffing when he threatened to eviscerate the media. "When he threatened to sue, when he mocked a disabled reporter, when he made clear his affinity for Vladimir Putin and Peter Thiel, he was issuing a warning." Dawes warned that U.S. journalists now need secure encryption of their devices to keep their sources safe "under a regime that has the most sophisticated surveillance capabilities ever imagined" and whose leader has a vindictive history.

Trump has found effective ways to bypass or manipulate the conventional media, largely through social media and friendly outlets, such as *Breitbart News*, but also by making provocative statements that inevitably generate traffic for mainstream outlets. During his campaign, *The Washington Post*'s Callum Borchers reported on preliminary talks about a dedicated Trump cable television channel that would enable him to bypass the conventional media altogether. Borchers described conservative Right Side Broadcasting Network as "the unofficial version of Trump TV since last summer" and noted that the campaign had "teamed up with Right Side to produce pre- and post-debate analysis shows that streamed on Trump's Facebook Page." After Trump chose Breitbart's chair, Stephen Bannon, as his chief White House strategist, some observers raised the specter of a "Trump *Pravda*," including *Politico*, which noted that *Breitbart* "could become the closest thing the United States has ever had to a 'state-run media enterprise,' to quote a phrase by a former *Breitbart* spokesman."

Though Trump made ample use of free media during the campaign, he has made it clear that he feels no need to accommodate or even tolerate conventional journalism. As a result, in Dawes's view, journalists will have to rely on their own investigations and sources or on Freedom of Information Act (FOIA) requests that are also growing increasingly problematic. U.S. journalists, Dawes wrote, can expect their FOIA requests to be further slowed—"walked to death or irrelevance, as they increasingly are in India, and other countries where the first flush of enthusiasm over FOIA legislation has [been] replaced with a deepening chill."

Dawes sees a particular parallel in India during the period after divisive Prime Minister Narendra Modi took power in 2002, when "journalists were banned from government offices they had once wandered freely. They were kicked off the presidential plane. Modi granted no interviews to the domestic press for over a year. His ministers and senior officials whispered privately that they had been ordered not to speak to the press." Among Dawes's other warnings is that conventional media outlets will see a financial incentive to "tack to the prevailing wind," which is something Minor recalled happening in Mississippi during the civil rights era, when many news outlets chose to embrace segregationist sentiments due to their own biases or to avoid isolation, reader backlash or the loss of advertising revenue.

Though Trump's power is more profound, he is hardly alone in his efforts; there are both those existing trends and the potential for trickle-down. On June 13, 2016, the same day that *The Washington Post* reported Trump had revoked its press credentials to his campaign events, the mayor of Harrisburg, Pennsylvania, Eric Papenfuse, ordered his spokesperson to cease communications with that city's largest news outlet, *The Patriot-News*/PennLive, and to bar its reporters from weekly city briefings following two stories the outlet ran that scrutinized his private business and real estate holdings. In December 2016, during protests over legislation passed by North Carolina's Republican supermajority legislature designed to strip the incoming Democratic governor of some of his powers, police demanded that all journalists, lobbyists and other members of the public leave the state House gallery, a public space. Among those who were subsequently arrested was Joe Killian, an investigative reporter for *N.C. Policy Watch*, an outlet of the advocacy group N.C. Justice Center, who was covering the protests. *The Huffington Post* later quoted Killian as saying, "I told them I didn't intend to leave. I was going to stay and continue to report the news. So they arrested me." Killian was charged with second-degree trespassing and breaking legislative building rules.

In a similar vein, in Minor's home state, a reporter for the nonpartisan, nonprofit news site *Mississippi Today* submitted a routine public records request that was followed by the adoption of a legislative rule to exempt all of its contracts from public scrutiny.

The *Mississippi Today* reporter, Kate Royals, was at the time covering a story about the legislature's hiring of a private firm to revamp the state's controversial educational funding program, and after she filed an official request for the contract, the legislature's House Management Committee passed a rule exempting legislative contracts from the state's open records law. "Even legislators could only view the documents—they couldn't copy them or share them," Royals said. In response, Royals queried the state attorney general, who informed the committee that the rule was illegal, and it was subsequently rescinded. Royals then received a copy of the contract, though the management committee chair informed her by email that the two developments were unrelated. Royals noted that the governor's office also ceased responding to requests for comment from *Mississippi Today*, following a reporter's pointed question about state poverty statistics in a census report. Such moves have made it more difficult to cover state government, she said. "It's definitely part of a larger attitude here. Obviously, it's not as dramatic as being jailed, but it's the same theme."

Minor recalled that even amid the notably hostile environment of 1960s Mississippi, independent reporters managed to have an impact. As an example, he recalled how an article he wrote about the creation of a state secret police force attracted national attention, after which the effort was abandoned. In another case, a confidential source provided him with a secret state report of local expenditures by race for every school district in the state. Minor's resulting article, which showed that in some districts $100 was budgeted for white students for every $1 budgeted for black students, got the attention of congressmen who used it to push for the 1964 Civil Rights Act.

But Minor said he's concerned that animosity toward the U.S. media is now broader in scope than during the civil rights era, and that although the federal government then provided a check on the rogue behavior of state officials and a sometimes-hostile public, "it looks like, not anymore."

Alan Huffman *is a freelance writer and editor and the author of five nonfiction books, most recently* Here I Am: The Story of Tim Hetherington, War Photographer.

5. Thwarting Freedom of Information

By Jason Leopold

UNCLASSIFIED

Exemption b (1)

(U) Offensive Foreign Counterintelligence Operations, 650th Military Intelligence Group (A-2012-0019-FMI)   Page 7

UNCLASSIFIED

A redacted document given to the author in response to one of his Freedom of Information Act requests.

(Jason Leopold)

O n December 13, 2016, I filed a Freedom of Information Act lawsuit against the FBI seeking a wide range of documents about a series of highly controversial decisions the bureau made in the weeks leading up to the U.S. presidential election that Democratic lawmakers and supporters of Hillary Clinton have claimed shifted support to her opponent, Donald Trump.

Most notably, FBI Director James Comey sent a letter to congressional leaders 10 days before the election alerting them that his agency's investigators may have uncovered new emails relevant to its probe of Clinton's email server and her handling of classified information. A long-dormant Twitter account operated by the FBI's records vault was also reactivated and tweeted newly posted records a week before the election about Bill Clinton's 2000 pardon of financier Marc Rich, which Comey had investigated when he was a U.S. attorney.

Was the FBI trying to help Trump get elected? Who in the bureau was leaking details about what was taking place behind the scenes to *The New York Times*, *The Wall Street Journal* and other outlets? That's what my FOIA lawsuit, which I filed as a VICE News reporter, aimed to find out. The goal was to gain access to documents that would lay bare decisions that led Comey to send his letter to Congress and explain why the FBI tweeted the Rich documents. But I'm not stopping there. My lawsuit also seeks everything the FBI has on *Breitbart News* and its chairman, Stephen Bannon.

Though the lawsuit is a direct response to the dramatic developments of the presidential election, it also underscores how government agencies stifle the flow of public information. My own immersion into the U.S. Freedom of Information Act began six years ago, when I received an urgent call from Mikey Weinstein, the head of a nonprofit group whose work focuses on enforcing the separation of church and state within the military.

Weinstein told me he had obtained a set of PowerPoint slides from a source in the U.S. Air Force that he wanted to share with me. He said the content was explosive and that, if I was interested, it would make for a very good story. I told him to send it over.

Later, as I thumbed through dozens of slides, it became apparent that these were very newsworthy documents. The PowerPoint laid bare how the Air Force trained nuclear missile officers on the ethics and morals of launching nuclear weapons by citing the teachings of Jesus Christ and Werner Von Braun, the father of the modern-day space program and a former Nazi SS soldier.

I wrote a story about it, with the documents embedded, that was published by Truthout.org. The response was swift and the impact huge. My report went viral, was picked up by other news outfits and, within 24 hours, led the Air Force to suspend its ethics training, which at the time had been in place for two decades. A couple of days later, the Air Force withdrew the training materials altogether.

Obviously, the story was dependent on that PowerPoint program. Documentation is the lifeblood of an investigative journalist, not only because it helps back up a story but because in many cases there is no story without it. Weinstein later informed me that one of his Air Force pals had used the Freedom of Information Act, commonly referred to as the FOIA, to retrieve the PowerPoint slides from the Air Force, which then verified their authenticity for me. His phone call not only gave me a scoop but also launched me on a professional odyssey that has produced reams of important documents in the years since.

The experience with the Air Force PowerPoint slides was a light bulb moment for me. I had spent years reporting on national security but faced increasing difficulty obtaining information about such issues from an administration that was highly secretive and aggressive in its pursuit of leaks to the media. And yet, a memorandum from then–President Barack Obama, issued on his first day in office, promised to usher in a new era of transparency and open government and instructed the heads of executive departments and agencies "to disclose information rapidly."

In the Air Force case, the FOIA provided a key mechanism for obtaining documents from a federal agency, so I decided to give it a try on other stories.

U.S. public records laws are the global standard, and many other countries look to America as an example. However, as I've pushed deeper into the realm, I've observed a countervailing trend: government agencies that seem intent on keeping me—and the public— in the dark, often by thwarting transparency requirements in what amounts to bureaucratic censorship, despite directives to the contrary from above and from state and federal transparency laws.

The same trend is unfolding in other countries. According to a 2011 Associated Press study, in which the wire service submitted open records requests to 105 countries with freedom of information laws, only a handful—14—responded within the time frame required by law. Thirty-eight other countries eventually answered most of the questions posted to them by the wire service and provided The Associated Press with some data. On average, younger democracies were far more responsive than older ones, the AP's analysis concluded, but at the same time, more than half never turned over any documents and three out of four didn't even acknowledge the AP's requests.

In the U.S., as agencies from the federal level down to the local level adapt to transparency requirements, many have formulated work-arounds—imposing exorbitant fees, arcane bureaucratic hurdles and discretionary exemptions to deny documents essential to breaking important stories. For a journalist whose appeals have failed, there is little recourse other than litigation, which is a significant barrier for freelancers who typically do not have the means for a potentially pro-tracted court battle.

The situation today is a marked departure from my experience with the Air Force story. In 2011, Weinstein connected me with his Air Force friend, who gave me a crash course in filing effective FOIA requests, and I studied the half-century-old law, the agencies' FOIA-specific regulations and their systems of record, where the documents I was seeking would likely be stored. I educated myself on how to con-vince agencies to grant me expedited processing (getting to the top of the pile) and to obtain fee waivers. Between 2011 and 2012, I fired off more than 500 FOIA requests on a wide range of subject matters, such as the CIA's targeted killing program, the treatment of detainees at Guantánamo and what appeared to be the FBI's surveillance and moni-toring of civil rights activists. What I learned from my Air Force men-tor is that, by creating a pipeline of requests early on, I would receive a steady flow of documents down the road, perhaps several times per week (and just as frequently, major scoops) once the agencies got around to processing my requests and producing responsive records.

I also began to observe that agencies often do not meet the letter of the law, which is something that is becoming more prevalent today. Though filing FOIAs has resulted in the disclosure of some important records, it has become less and less practical in application as a result of bureaucratic fees and backlogs that extend years in some cases.

The FOIA requires an agency to make a determination on releasing records within 20 business days, with an extension of 10 business days available in "unusual circumstances." Unfortunately, very few FOIA requests are decided within the time frame required by the law, and delayed responses are a significant problem for investigative journalists. The information sought may become less valuable over time, such as information about a candidate that will be less newsworthy after the election is over and information about a war that will be less relevant after the conflict ends. Often, information delayed is information denied.

Making matters worse, agencies take a narrow view of which circumstances merit expedited processing of FOIA requests. For example, the Defense Intelligence Agency denied my request in 2013 for expedited processing for documents related to the harm to national security caused by Edward Snowden's revelations, although it was a matter of great public interest. And even when expedited processing is granted, the process moves slowly. In 2014, I submitted a FOIA request to the Department of Justice for records relating to the agency's investigation of allegations that the CIA had accessed the computers of staffers working for the Senate Intelligence Committee without authorization. Although expedited processing was granted, the agency decided it would not release any records until January 29, 2016. When the agency finally released the documents, they were revealing, to say the least, and had an enormous impact. The resulting 9,000-word article took months to investigate and write. It centered on allegations that the CIA spied on Senate staffers who conducted the probe into the torture program. Senator Dianne Feinstein first leveled those charges against the CIA in March 2014 during a stunning floor speech. At the time, CIA Director John Brennan said Feinstein's allegations were preposterous. The result was an ongoing argument—so contentious that it led to a near constitutional crisis—which played out in the media during much of 2015.

Through my FOIA efforts, about 500 pages of related documents were declassified, revealing many new details about the spying incident. It proved that Feinstein was correct: The CIA did snoop on Senate staffers' work and violated a 2009 agreement between the agency and the committee. Those documents also suggested that a January 2015 CIA accountability review board report that exonerated CIA employees responsible for accessing Senate computers was a cover-up.

One of the documents in the cache was an apology letter CIA Director Brennan had drafted to Feinstein and the committee's ranking Republican, Senator Saxby Chambliss—a letter that Brennan never sent. When we asked the CIA about the letter, we were told that it had been mistakenly turned over to us. The agency urged us not to publicize it because it was embarrassing. We denied the request. It was a rare agency FOIA snafu.

Our reporting on the CIA documents, supplemented with interviews we conducted with key Senate staffers and members of the committee, also contained an explosive new revelation: A Google search conducted by a Senate Intelligence Committee staffer was the catalyst behind the CIA's breach into the committee's computers. Our investigative report on one of America's most contentious clashes related to oversight in decades sparked a national discussion about the separation of powers and led to calls for accountability of CIA officials by both Feinstein and Senator Ron Wyden. And the FOIA was the reason we were able to do it.

It's important to note that I would never have obtained these documents had I not litigated. Agencies often ignored both Obama's original memorandum and then–Attorney General Eric Holder's official FOIA guidelines, which he sent to the heads of the executive departments and agencies. Holder's guidelines, contained in a March 19, 2009, memo, could not be any clearer: "An agency should not withhold information simply because it may do so legally. I strongly encourage agencies to make discretionary disclosures of information. An agency should not withhold records merely because it can demonstrate, as a technical matter, that the records fall within the scope of a FOIA exemption."

The question, of course, is what sort of guidelines may be issued by the Trump administration, given the president's antipathy toward the press and the fact that agencies routinely ignored even his predecessor's directives.

In many cases, agencies thwart requests by invoking Exemption 5, or (b)(5), otherwise known as the "withhold it because you can" exemption. Exemption 5 applies to records that are part of the behind-the-scenes decision-making process—called "deliberative"—and covers any "inter-agency or intra-agency memorandums or letters." This is a discretionary exemption that government agencies are free to waive in favor of disclosure, though they rarely do. What ends up happening is that either a requester receives documents that are heavily redacted or the documents are withheld in their entirety. Agencies have frequently used Exemption 5 to hide misdeeds by claiming they were inter- or intra-agency communications. The most egregious example, perhaps, is when the CIA denied the National Security Archive's request for a 30-year-old draft volume of the Bay of Pigs, even though four previous volumes were released without any harm to national security or deliberations within the government. The CIA further argued, oddly, that the release of this volume would "confuse the public" as to whether the document was official CIA history.

Another recurring problem that journalists experience is with the FBI's invocation of Exemption 7(A). Under this exemption, an agency may withhold "records or information" compiled for law enforcement purposes, which "could reasonably be expected to interfere with enforcement proceedings." The exemption comes up frequently in my work because I often request records or information about recent events.

Congress deliberately chose the words "records or information" when it amended Exemption 7 in 1974 to eliminate a blank exemption for investigatory files compiled for law enforcement purposes. The problem had been that agencies could simply place documents that they wanted to withhold from disclosure inside an investigatory file and then treat the document as exempted simply because of its location. In that way, agencies managed to work around the transparency requirements.

Despite Congress's clear intention and the plain language of FOIA in the 1974 amendment, the FBI continues to withhold information where the record requested "is located in an investigative file which is exempt from disclosure pursuant to 5 U.S.C. 552(b)(7)(A)." I have received dozens of denial letters from the FBI based on this erroneous interpretation of the FOIA, and the Department of Justice's Office of Information Policy has affirmed the FBI's decision in every administrative appeal I have filed. The FBI has not defended its position in court but instead conducts a new review applying the proper standard once litigation has commenced. As a result, the issue becomes moot. In other words, the FBI *will* search for segregable records located in an investigative file, but you have to sue the bureau first.

A common FOIA complaint among journalists, especially freelancers whose funds are limited, is that agencies also often charge astronomical fees in an effort to deter requesters from filing requests and obtaining records. This practice is rampant on the state level and very difficult to overcome. In 2014, for example, I sought emails from officials with the city of Ferguson, Missouri, that mentioned or referred to the shooting death of unarmed African-American teenager Michael Brown. The city clerk told me that I would have to pay $2,000 in advance for a search to be conducted and to pay the city attorney to review and redact any responsive emails. Clearly, this was an attempt to discourage me from accessing public records. I told the clerk that these records were in the public interest, given the widespread media attention surrounding Brown's case, and that I, as a journalist, should be granted a fee waiver. I filed an appeal over the exorbitant fees with Ferguson city clerk Megan Asikainen. She told me in an email that my appeal was denied "because the fees are necessary in order to provide the materials you requested." In other words, it didn't matter that I would be informing the public. She further explained that the $2,000 was "based on an estimate of the City's programming costs related to the extensive request and the research time related to the documents that may be responsive to the request."

So my news outlet, VICE News, agreed to cut the city a check, essentially calling the city's bluff. When the search was completed, we ended up with only seven emails, but they were newsworthy, revealing that police officers in the city viewed themselves as victims. Officers stated that they feared that people in the community were "gunning" for them and that officers were having a "rough" time dealing with the news media.

On the federal level, there's a misconception among journalists that by simply filing a FOIA request and stating "I'm a journalist," they won't be charged fees. But when fee waivers are denied, it's usually because a journalist fails to state in their initial request how they intend to use the records and show that disclosure is "likely to contribute significantly to public understanding of the operations or activities of the government." The burden is on the journalist to include language in a request articulating why he or she should be granted a waiver of fees and that they have the ability to convey the information to a broad segment of the public. Too often, journalists throw up their hands when told that the records they seek will cost hundreds or thousands of dollars. The FOIA provides for appealing a fee waiver denial, and in my experience, it's usually granted when you take the time to answer these questions. But the time line invariably gets stretched out, which may affect the news value of the story.

Even when a journalist acts with the utmost diligence in filing a FOIA request, agency foot-dragging can and often frustrates their attempt to obtain records at the time when they are needed most. In most cases, filing a lawsuit moves the request to the top of the pile and catalyzes the release of documents. That's certainly been my experience over the past six years. However, not all investigative journalists are in a position to expend the substantial resources necessary to bring FOIA lawsuits, and even large media outlets may conclude that the cost of litigation outweighs the benefits.

All of which means that, despite specific directives from the former president and attorney general and transparency efforts in Congress and state legislatures, agencies from the Department of Defense down to the local city clerk's office frequently and increasingly find ways to use the rules in the service of de facto censorship. Given that the U.S. sets the standard for public document availability, that is discouraging and doubtless prevents crucial stories from seeing the light of day.

Yet there may be some hope. In early 2016, a few weeks before the 50th anniversary of the passage of the Freedom of Information Act, Congress passed legislation to reform the act, and President Obama signed it into law shortly thereafter. The new law is supposed to make it easier for journalists, historians and the general public to gain access to documents by forcing government agencies to be more transparent. The bill will codify into law Obama's original presidential memorandum instructing all government agencies to "adopt a presumption in favor of disclosure, in order to renew their commitment to the principles embodied in FOIA, and to usher in a new era of open Government."

Most important, the reform bill overhauled Exemption 5, the "withhold it because you can" exemption. When government agencies cite Exemption 5, which applies only to internal deliberations, they can withhold records under that exemption forever. But under the new law, federal agencies can only withhold records pertaining to internal deliberations for 25 years. For historians, that's a significant change. Government agencies are required to issue new regulations explaining how they intend to implement the new reforms to the FOIA, which they are currently doing. But the bill does not contain any additional funding to assist government agencies with carrying out the reforms. That means long delays will persist and agencies will no doubt attempt to exploit loopholes to keep the public in the dark.

Jason Leopold *is an Emmy-nominated investigative reporter and correspondent for BuzzFeed News, where he reports on national security.*

Case in Point

By Michael Pell

I n December 2010, Robin Gordon faced an ultimatum. She had found that a debt collection company had purchased a $291 tax lien on an apartment she owned in Atlanta, Georgia, after her mortgage company failed to pay a small portion of her Fulton County taxes five years earlier. Now, she could either pay the debt collection company $8,200, a 2,700 percent increase, or the sheriff's office would auction her apartment to pay the debt.

Eventually, Gordon's mortgage company agreed to pay, but for the *Atlanta Journal Constitution*, her experience raised a host of questions. How many tax liens had the Fulton County tax commissioner sold to private companies over the years? Who bought them? And how many people lost their homes over small bills and clerical oversights?

At first, an official from the tax commissioner's office said they couldn't answer any of these questions because they didn't track lien sales.

Days later, an attorney representing Fulton County said they did track lien sales using a property transaction database maintained by the tax commissioner's office.

And so began the parry-and-thrust dynamic of a two-year records battle that saw the county employ some of the most common tactics used by government agencies across the United States— and the globe—to frustrate records requests.

(continued)

(continued)

Freedom of information laws, which include the right to file requests under the Freedom of Information Act (FOIA) in the U.S., are increasingly popular around the world, even in some fairly repressive countries, because they represent good public relations regarding transparency and open government. Theoretically, at least, such laws ensure access to public records; yet, their practical utility can be thwarted through bureaucratic foot-dragging, what are essentially dumps of reams of useless documents that are impossible to sift through, or exorbitant fees.

Though the Fulton County battle took place in 2010 and 2011, it remains an extreme example of a practice that has become widespread, which has the effect of killing stories by making access to the necessary public records significantly difficult, if not impossible.

In December 2010, while working for the Atlanta newspaper, I requested county records detailing the number of liens it had sold. The county denied the request on the grounds that there were no records responsive to the request, essentially saying that while the tax commissioner knew how many liens were sold each year, the information had never been committed to a report, email, or any other written document.

In response, the newspaper (typically known by its acronym, the *AJC*) issued a request in January 2011 for the tax commissioner's entire property transaction database.

Later that month, Fulton County came back with a cost estimate for processing the records request. Government agencies often use inflated and vague processing fees as a barrier to access, knowing the modern media has a limited budget to purchase records, but Fulton took the tactic to an extreme.

The county attorney's office said they would have to print each record from the database. At 25 cents a page, it would cost the *AJC* $16.2 million for the 64.8 million records. Parry.

Not only is the cost an insurmountable barrier, but Fulton would only make the records available in paper, a format that made any meaningful analysis impossible. Providing records as paper or a PDF is another common practice for government agencies looking to stymie access to public records.

While this would be enough to permanently stall many records requests, the *AJC* lobbied the Georgia legislature to strengthen the state's open records law and close loopholes like those that allowed state agencies and municipal governments to deny requests for digital records.

After bolstering the open records law and using open records requests to learn the name of the database and the name of the company that developed it, the *AJC* submitted a new records request in May 2012. Thrust.

Days later, Fulton County denied the request yet again, this time claiming that portions of the data were trade secrets of the software company. Parry.

At the nexus of government and private business interests, this is another common and potentially fatal response to a records request.

But the *AJC* filed a complaint with the Georgia attorney general's office and convinced them to get involved. Ultimately, it was only the threat of a lawsuit from the state attorney general's office that compelled the Fulton County Tax Commissioner's Office to turn over the database two years after the initial request.

An analysis of the database revealed that one company purchased $350 million worth of liens over a 10-year period. The data also showed the company received favorable treatment from the tax commissioner's office. The tax commissioner sold the company liens when other companies were told liens were not for sale and helped the company make up to $20 million in additional revenue by allowing the company to charge property owners a 10 percent penalty that would otherwise be collected by the county.

"It's very unfortunate that it took so much time to do what was right and it's very unfortunate that it took a letter saying that suit would come within 10 days," then–Attorney General Sam Olens told the *AJC* in 2013. "That's not the way the Open Records Act is supposed to work."

(*continued*)

(continued)

R. DAVID WARE
COUNTY ATTORNEY

TELEPHONE (404) 612-0246
FACSIMILE (404) 730-6324

FULTON COUNTY

December 15, 2010

VIA U.S. MAIL and EMAIL
Michael B. Pell
Atlanta Journal Constitution
223 Perimeter Center Pkwy.
Atlanta, GA 30346

            Re: Open Records Request

Dear Mr. Pell:

    The Tax Commissioner's Office received a copy of your open records request dated December 10, 2010 on December 13, 2010. In said correspondence, you have requested the following records:

- The total number of delinquent properties that had their tax liens sold in 2007, 2008, and 2009.
- The total dollar value for the delinquent properties that had their tax liens sold in 2007, 2008, and 2009.

    The Tax Commissioner's Office has reviewed your request and has found that it does not maintain an existing document, in electronic version or otherwise, which shows the **total** number of delinquent properties that had their tax liens sold in 2007, 2008 and 2009 or the **total** dollar value for the delinquent properties that had their tax liens sold in 2007, 2008 and 2009 and the dollar amount due for delinquent properties for tax years 2007, 2008 and 2009. In order to produce the records requested, the Tax Commissioner's Office would have to generate reports by querying system records and tables, and then perform comparisons of those reports in order to produce accurate results. These tasks are outside the normal business functions for the Tax Commissioner's Office and would require dedicated hours and staffing to meet the request. As previously stated in response to your Open Records Request dated November 30, 2010, the Tax Commissioner does maintain a physical copy of each lien transferred by the Tax Commissioner for tax years 2007, 2008 and 2009. Each of these liens contains the amount of the taxes, fees and penalties owed by the defendant in fi. fa. The documentation maintained by the Tax Commissioner's Office is available for review by appointment.

    A fee is charged for the time it takes to search, retrieve, copy and supervise access to the requested documents pursuant to O.C.G.A. § 50-18-71(d) and (f). However, no fee will be assessed for the first fifteen (15) minutes of this search. If you should request printed copies or request further documentation pursuant to this request, an administrative fee will be charged. This fee is set at the hourly rate of the lowest paid full-time employee within each department with the necessary skill and training to respond to your request. You will also be of $.25 per page for each printed page of the documents you request. Please note that the total amount for searching and retrieving and/or copying all documents is due upon release.

Please direct all inquiries regarding this request to the Office of the Fulton County Attorney to my attention. If you have any questions, please feel free to contact me at 404-612-0246.

Sincerely

W. Shannon Sams
Staff Attorney

WSS/deh

xc: Dr. Arthur E. Ferdinand, Tax Commissioner
       Matthew C. Welch, Senior Attorney

★ ★ ★

OFFICE OF THE FULTON COUNTY ATTORNEY
141 PRYOR STREET, S.W.
SUITE 4038
ATLANTA, GEORGIA 30303

R. DAVID WARE
COUNTY ATTORNEY

FULTON COUNTY

TELEPHONE (404) 612-0246
FACSIMILE (404) 730-6324

January 28, 2011

VIA U.S. MAIL and EMAIL
Michael B. Pell
Atlanta Journal Constitution
223 Perimeter Center Pkwy.
Atlanta, GA 30346

Re: Open Records Request

Dear Mr. Pell:

The Tax Commissioner's Office received a copy of your Open Records request dated January 14, 2011 on January 18, 2011. In said correspondence, you requested the following information:

(continued)

The database containing information on all fi fas issued by the county. I am asking for the entire database. This database was referenced by W. Shannon Sams, staff attorney with the Fulton County attorney's office, in a statement issued to The Atlanta Journal-Constitution December 17, 2010. Mr. Sams also referenced the database in a December 20th email: "The computer system used by the Tax Commissioner's Office would have to be manipulated in order to create such a report."

In response to the referenced Open Records Request, the Tax Commissioner's Office indicated in correspondence dated January 21, 2011 that they would not be able to provide an immediate estimate of the volume of documentation to be produced or a timeline and estimated cost of such production due to the exceptional volume of data requested. The Tax Commissioner's Office, however, stated in its original response to your request that such estimate would be available by January 28, 2011. I write today as a follow-up to the referenced correspondence of January 21, 2011.

After consulting with IT and the Tax Commissioner, it has been determined that responsive information exists and can be produced; however, significant portions of the database you have requested will have to be redacted in order to comply with the security exemptions set forth under O.C.G.A. § 50-18-72 of the open records act including the addresses, social security numbers and email addresses for judges, public employees, teachers, police officers, EMTs, and other officials or exempt classes. Specifically, these exemptions are set forth in O.C.G.A. § 50-18-72(a)(1); O.C.G.A. § 50-18-72(a)(11.3)(A); O.C.G.A. § 50-18-72(a)(11.3)(E); O.C.G.A. § 50-18-72(a)(13); O.C.G.A. § 50-18-72(a)(13.1); O.C.G.A. § 50-18-72(b)(1); and O.C.G.A. § 50-18-72(e)(3). IT has informed the Tax Commissioner that such exempt information cannot be redacted in electronic form without IT producing a report or creating data tables not currently in existence. As you know, the Open Records Act does not require the creation of reports or documents that are not in existence. As such, the information responsive to this request can only be provided in printed form. IT estimates that a printout of all requested information in the database will comprise approximately 64,800,000 (sixty-four million, eight hundred thousand) pages. Please note that the Open Records Act allows a fee of $.25 per page for each printed page, meaning that production of the requested documents would cost approximately $16,200,00.00 (Sixteen Million, Two-Hundred Thousand Dollars). However, please understand that due to the volume and complexity of complying with this request, this estimate may need to be amended during the process of producing the responsive documentation. Of course, we will promptly notify you of any changes in costs as soon as this information becomes available.

Should you elect to request that this data be produced at this juncture, an additional fee will be charged for the time it takes to search, retrieve, print and supervise access to the requested information pursuant to O.C.G.A. § 50-18-71(d) and (f). However, no fee will be assessed for the first fifteen (15) minutes of this search. As indicated in our initial response letter, it is expected that both a system analyst and programming analyst from IT will be needed in order to produce the data requested. An employee in the Tax Commissioner's Office with knowledge of the systems database will also need to be consulted in order to assist in producing the data requested. The applicable hourly fee for the IT system analyst is $32.36 per hour. The applicable rate for the person in the Tax Commissioner's Office responsible for assisting with your Open Records request is $50.38 per hour. Given the extreme volume of materials requested, however, it is impossible to estimate the time needed to produce such documents at this juncture.

Should you elect to have the requested documents printed, considerable additional time will be required to redact such documents. As indicated above, the exemptions set forth in O.C.G.A. § 50-18-72(a)(1), O.C.G.A. § 50-18-72(a)(11.3)(A), O.C.G.A. § 50-18-72(a)(11.3)(E), O.C.G.A. § 50-18-72(a)(13), O.C.G.A. § 50-18-72(a)(13.1), O.C.G.A. § 50-18-72(b)(1), and

O.C.G.A. § 50-18-72(e)(3) require that the addresses, social security numbers and email addresses for certain classes of individuals be redacted from public records produced in response to an Open Records Request. Again, given the extreme volume of materials requested, it is impossible to estimate the time needed to redact such documents at this juncture.

Please direct all inquiries regarding this request to the Office of the Fulton County Attorney to either my attention or to the attention of W. Shannon Sams, including any requests to modify or narrow this request. You may contact us at 404-612-0246.

Sincerely,

Matthew C. Welch
Senior Attorney

MCW/deh

xc: Dr. Arthur E. Ferdinand, Tax Commissioner
        Ryan Fernandes, Director of Information Technology
        Terry Noble, Tax Administrator
        W. Shannon Sams, Staff Attorney

P:\CAOpenRecords\TaxCom\Supplemental Response to Request dated 1.14.11 mcw.doc

Michael Pell is a reporter on the Reuters data team who covers topics ranging from healthcare fraud to workplace safety.

6. Disrupting the Debate

By Alexandra Ellerbeck

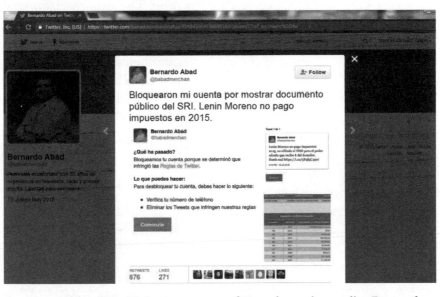

A screen shot of the Twitter account of Ecuadoran journalist Bernardo Abad. An English translation of his tweet reads: "They blocked my account for showing public documents from the internal revenue service (SRI). Lenin Moreno didn't pay taxes in 2015.

(CPJ)

On July 10, 2016, Ecuadoran journalist Bernardo Abad tweeted that the former vice president of Ecuador, Lenin Moreno, had not paid income taxes for the year before. A week later, Abad received a message from Twitter saying his account had been blocked for violating its terms of service. Within 24 hours, at least five others' accounts were temporarily suspended after they tweeted about Moreno's taxes. By the end of the week, nine accounts had been temporarily suspended, according to the freedom of expression advocacy group Fundamedios. Twitter declined to comment on the suspensions.

Free speech organizations have argued that Ecuador's disappearing content and suspended accounts are the direct result of a government campaign to censor critical information. The groups claim this is part of a broader global pattern—that censoring or drowning out critical voices is no longer the exclusive activity of authoritarian governments, such as China and Russia, but is also being done in Ecuador and Mexico.

Moreno, who was lauded for his work on disability rights in Ecuador after he was shot in the back during a carjacking and paralyzed from the waist down, later served as the U.N. Special Envoy on Disability and Accessibility in Geneva. He is the likely candidate to run for president on the ticket of the ruling party after President Rafael Correa's term ends next year. Much of the Twitter chatter concerned a recent report by the investigative news site Fundación Mil Hojas (1,000 Pages Foundation) that revealed Moreno earned more than US$1 million during two years in Geneva when he was working as a special envoy there. Moreno said in a Facebook chat message that the Vienna Convention on Diplomatic Relations exempted him from paying taxes on this money because he was a special envoy.

The nine Twitter suspensions that followed reports on Moreno's taxes coincided with eight more account disruptions (suspensions or forced removal of tweets) in July 2016 among activists who criticized the government in other ways, according to information provided by Fundamedios. Moreno denied making takedown requests for any of the disruptions, and Twitter did not respond to a request for comment. After Fundamedios, the Committee to Protect Journalism and other organizations appealed to Twitter, the accounts were restored.

Ecuadoran free expression groups have long complained that opposition activists and critical journalists risk having their Twitter accounts suspended due to fishy copyright or terms of service complaints. Fundamedios says it documented at least 806 notifications against 292 accounts filed between mid-April and mid-July of 2016, most of them by a single Spanish company called Ares Rights that has routinely filed requests on behalf of Ecuadoran government agencies or politicians.

CPJ has been unable to independently verify those numbers, but reports of censorship on social media have been widespread in Ecuador. In 2013, *Buzzfeed* received a copyright notification from Ares Rights, filed on behalf of Ecuador's National Intelligence Secretariat, after the media outlet published leaked documents alleging that the agency had purchased surveillance equipment. Ares Rights has also filed a number of takedown requests on behalf of the Ecuadoran Secretary of Communications (SECOM) against free speech organizations and opposition media outlets, despite the fact that the government agency has denied any contractual relationship with the company in the past. SECOM did not respond to requests for comment.

During the Arab Spring six years ago, social media was seen as an organic expression of popular opinion that was capable of undermining governments and sparking revolutions. While the narrative of the social media revolution has become complicated in the years since, the general idea was, and in many places still is, that social media provides a snapshot of the public's conversation. It is this assumption that leads to controversy when social media platforms step out of the background and appear to exert editorial influence.

But it is not just the platforms that are influencing content: The governments that these networks of citizen journalists were supposed to check have become increasingly sophisticated in using social media for surveillance, censorship and propaganda. Governments and high-profile political figures are, for better or worse, increasingly shaping the debates taking place on platforms such as Twitter and Facebook, whether through armies of propaganda artists in Russia, China and Mexico, the surveillance and removal of accounts as part of the United States' counterterrorism efforts or the suspension of critical Twitter accounts in Ecuador.

Twitter publishes annual transparency reports about the number of takedown demands the company receives from government agencies or courts throughout the world. Between January and June 2016, those reports found that Russia had 1,601 requests, Turkey had 2,493 and the United States had 100, though Twitter said it did not comply with the vast majority of the removal requests. Ecuador only had one request, with which Twitter said it did not comply, in contrast with the frequent complaints of allegedly politically motivated copyright and privacy violation complaints, which are harder to detect or to link directly to the government.

■ ■ ■

On December 1, 2014, journalist Erin Gallagher was blogging about a major protest in Mexico City. She had been following the case of a group of missing Mexican students since September 26, 2014, when the 43 students from the Ayotzinapa Rural Teachers' College disappeared on their way to a protest in the capital Mexico City. A flawed investigation, and indications that the military might have been involved, stoked existing frustrations with violence and corruption in the country and sparked a series of massive protests. Gallagher covered the demonstrations remotely from her home in Pennsylvania for the website Revolution News by talking to activists and following social media. She said she was following the protest-linked hashtag #RompeElMiedo (Break the Fear), when something strange happened.

"I had been following the protest live all day long and into the evening, and then all of a sudden the hashtag I was following was flooded with spam," Gallagher said. "When you run into it online in real time, you know that there's something strange happening. It's obvious that it's not organic information." Posts connected to the hashtag were filled with nonsense, random words or symbols, to the point that it became unusable.

Gallagher said that she realized she had run into political bots—automated social media bots programmed to influence online discussions. Researchers who study online bots confirm that there is evidence that trolls, or bots, manipulate social media in Mexico in order to change trending topics, threaten journalists, push out propaganda or divert online discussions that are critical of certain political figures.

"I would say that Mexico is the benchmark for the worst and most manipulative use of bots," said Sam Woolley, the project manager of Politicalbots.org. "Bots are used as a roadblock," he said. "A bunch of information would be tweeted at activists with the goal of disrupting conversations or having a chilling effect."

Nicknamed Peñabots for their tendency to send messages in favor of Mexican President Enrique Peña Nieto or his party, experts told CPJ that bots were now being used by all political factions in Mexico. Gallagher said the general assumption that bots are active in Mexico's political discussions is so widespread that some legitimate expressions of support for the government may be mischaracterized as spam.

Bots are not always easy to identify. Although there are some indicators, such as the frequency of messages, the coherence of messages and the relationships between bots, it can be hard to definitively identify automatic accounts, especially for casual observers. And bots are becoming increasingly sophisticated. "For any detection system you write, I can write a bot that gets around it," said Tim Hwang, a researcher at the New York City–based research institute Data and Society. "I think it will be an arms race. Campaigns of manipulation will get more sophisticated."

In Mexico, Woolley said that it is increasingly common to see bots combined with human commentators. A bot account might initiate a discussion, but then a human will take over if anyone else becomes engaged in a back and forth.

Hwang and Woolley are both quick to point out that politically oriented bots are not always bad. They can be used to connect political activists, provide information or track incidents. For example, there is a bot that tracks every shooting by a police officer in the United States. Still, they are subject to being abused.

Even harder than identifying political bots is figuring out who is paying for them and where they come from. In March, Bloomberg cited jailed Colombian hacker Andrés Sepúlveda as saying he was hired by Peña Nieto's campaign for president in 2012 and that one of his tasks was to manipulate online opinion by managing fake profiles and an army of 30,000 Twitter bots. Although Bloomberg said that parts of Sepúlveda's narrative coincided with technical attacks and propaganda that took place during the election campaign, not every detail of his story was independently corroborated. The Office of the Presidency did not respond to requests for comment.

Political manipulation is hardly centered in Ecuador or Mexico. A survey of 65 countries in the 2015 edition of Freedom House's report, "Freedom on the Net," found that 24 of them employed the use of pro-government commentators to manipulate discussion. In China, a group of government workers known as the "Fifty Cent Party" posts pro-government propaganda and coordinates smear campaigns against critics, while armies of government-linked commentators have viciously attacked journalists in Russia. Even the United States has researched social media manipulation for counterterrorism efforts.

Manipulation is also not limited to Twitter. Woolley and Hwang said there are bots and paid trolls on Facebook and other platforms as well. The open structure of Twitter simply makes it easier to detect.

For journalists, manipulation of social media means that some discussions are lost while others are added under false pretenses. These are difficult territories to chart. Even as Ecuadoran journalists persistently republish, again and again, censored content, and Mexican journalists soldier on in the face of trolling and threats, governments and political operatives continue to expand and adapt their efforts to thwart public debate and opposition.

Alexandra Ellerbeck is a research associate in CPJ's Americas program who previously worked at Freedom House and was a Fulbright teaching fellow at the State University of Pará in Brazil.

7. Discredited

By Yaqiu Wang

A Chinese investor monitors stock prices at a brokerage in Beijing in February, 2016. Authorities have announced a plan to score individuals' "social credibility."

(AP/Ng Han Guan)

I n what would be a uniquely daunting form of censorship, the Chinese government is making plans to link journalists' financial credibility to their online posts.

The creation of China's system of credit scoring, which will be implemented in stages, could result in scenarios in which journalists who write or speak critically of the government face direct, personal financial consequences. Those consequences could be life-altering: A journalist whose social media post is deemed a "rumor" by the government could see her credit score lowered, resulting in her being denied a loan or saddled with a high interest rate.

The impacts could also be more mundane, such as if the same journalist attempted to sell a secondhand bicycle on Taobao, China's equivalent to Amazon, only to find the prospective buyer backing out due to trust issues related to her low credit score.

Neither of these scenarios would stem directly from the journalist's financial history but would be directly triggered by a critical online post.

When most people talk about credit scores, they refer to a system in which a person's credit ranking is determined by how well she pays her bills and other debts. That is not the case in China's impending system of credit scoring.

In June 2014, the State Council, the administrator of the Chinese central government, issued a planning document that sets forth the creation of a nationwide "Social Credit System" to monitor and rate the "social credibility" of individuals, private companies, government agencies and nongovernmental organizations based on information from various government agencies and private institutions. Such information could include criminal records, tax documents, employer evaluations, purchasing preferences and online activities. The document states that the system would evaluate the credit history and online activities of internet users and blacklist "individuals engaging in online swindles" and "rumormongering." The document also calls for adopting "measures against subjects listed on black lists," including restricting their online activities, barring sectoral access and reporting them to corresponding departments for exposure.

The stated goal of the Social Credit System is to reward trustworthiness and punish "breaking trust" throughout Chinese society.

Trustworthiness, under the proposed system, would be decided by a government that has a history of censoring free speech.

"To link online rumor-mongering with one's social credit score can just be another way to punish government critics for speaking up," said New York–based blogger Wen Yunchao, who left China in 2012 after being repeatedly harassed by police over his online writing. Regarding the possible ramifications of the credit score proposal, he noted, "If you post 'rumor'—or negative information about the Chinese government—online, your credit score becomes lower as a result. It may affect you in real life, such as you have to pay a higher interest rate when applying for a house loan, or you can be barred from taking the civil service exam or bar exam or from working for the state media. Of course, the current system has not expanded to this degree yet, but from the design and implementation of the system, I see a high possibility of such linkage."

The planning document, which brims with political rhetoric, is unspecific about certain key issues, such as the grounds for blacklisting, how the government would collect the data and how the scores would be used by businesses and individuals. Given that China has about 1.4 billion people, the challenges to implementing such a system would be significant, but so too are its potential ramifications.

Since the document was drafted in 2014, various levels and departments of the Chinese government have been collectively pushing for its implementation, as illustrated by numerous articles published by state media and policy documents issued by the government. For example, in July 2016, the Communist Youth League, a youth organization of the Communist Party with more than 80 million members, promulgated the Youth Credit System Building Plan (2016–2020), which lays out specific objectives to be reached by 2020, measures of implementation and areas of focus. The eighth point of focus is "travel and tourism" and states, "encourage public cultural and sports facilities—including museums, public libraries and sports stadiums—and public parks, tourist sites, and other places to provide preferential treatment to trustworthy youth. Encourage transportation companies to provide ticket purchasing preferential policies to trustworthy youth. Encourage airlines to promote 'honest plane tickets,' providing trustworthy volunteers with 'credit purchasing,' priority services and other preferential measures." It is similar to the 2014 planning document in that it lacks an explanation for how youth credit scores will be determined.

Utilizing the Social Credit System would require accurately pinning down and linking every online activity to the person behind it, which could be done using an online identification technology called eID, a Chinese innovation, according to research by Chinese scholars.

An eID is a smart chip that can be loaded onto SIM cards, bank cards and identity cards and used to authenticate a user's identity online without revealing personal information, significantly lessening the potential for theft or alteration of the information, according to the Chinese government.

In recent years, the Chinese government has attempted to enforce real-name registration on different online platforms, including social media, mobile apps, e-commerce websites and live video streaming, with varying success. The research arm of the Ministry of Public Security, which has been developing eID technology for several years, announced in June 2016 that it has "established the preliminary eID online identification infrastructure and service system." The use of eID, when fully implemented, will enable the Chinese government to know precisely who is doing what online.

In June 2015, the State Information Center launched a website called Credit China on which people can search companies' and individuals' credit histories. The Committee to Protect Journalists' test of the system shows that the current data set primarily involves business records, such as who has dodged taxes, broken business contracts or failed to follow court rulings. The system is expected to soon include data on people and entities in other areas as well. In a February 2015 document, the Beijing government stated that establishing credit records for "news media personnel" is a priority during its process of implementing the central government's policy directives.

Journalists and observers familiar with the Chinese media have decried what they see as a system riddled with corruption, in which direct payment for positive news and extortion are rampant. Those who spoke with CPJ said a system that exposes dishonest behavior and highlights journalists who uphold media ethics is not intrinsically a bad idea but that such a system could easily be manipulated to monitor journalists and force them into self-censorship.

The Chinese government has in recent years vigorously pursued efforts to curtail what it considers to be online rumormongering. In 2013, China's top court and prosecutor ruled that people who post libelous information viewed more than 5,000 times or reposted more than 500 times can be charged with defamation and jailed for up to three years. Sharing false information deemed to cause "serious social disorder" can result in a maximum five-year jail term.

Accusing journalists and bloggers of spreading rumors is a tactic often used to punish those who report critically on the Chinese government. Among many such cases, *New Express* reporter Liu Hu spent a year in jail after being detained in August 2013 for allegedly "fabricating and spreading rumors" while exposing the corrupt dealings of a government official on his Weibo account, China's Twitter-like social media platform. Wang Xiaolu, a financial reporter for the business magazine *Caijing*, was kept in police custody from August 2015 to February 2016 for "fabricating and spreading false information" after he reported on fluctuations in the Chinese financial market.

Journalists told CPJ the online credit system is a significant concern because it represents a new way of linking a person's speech with other aspects of their lives. Censorship in China already goes beyond the usual tactics of removing journalists' and writers' social media accounts, shutting down news websites and jailing journalists; it also involves thwarting journalists' other daily activities, denying them career opportunities and banishing them from mainstream social engagements.

Wu Wei, known by his pen name Ye Du, is a writer and editor for the Independent Chinese PEN Center website, which reports on and documents human rights issues in China. Ye told CPJ that in addition to being frequently harassed by the police and detained for three months in 2012, he lost business opportunities due to his writing.

"In 2006, a lawyer in Guangzhou [province] wanted to partner with me to found an internet-based business project," Ye said. "After learning this, the police immediately went to his law firm to warn him, forced his landlord to evict him, and ordered his clients to sever ties with him. Under such pressure, he had no choice but to forgo the partnership with me." (CPJ was unable to independently verify this claim.) Ye also said that in 2011, around the time of his detention, the police told his neighbors in his apartment complex to cease contact with him, and he has been barred from purchasing train tickets and staying in hotels during sensitive events, such as the anniversaries of the Tiananmen Square massacre.

After spending a year in prison, enduring numerous interrogations, being pressured to give confessions on state television, being barred from applying for compensation for his wrongful imprisonment and being censored on social media, Liu Hu found it difficult to find work. "The Chinese government ordered news organizations not to work with me," Liu said. "Reputable news outlets didn't want to employ me. After I freelanced for several news outlets, the Cyberspace Administration Office [China's internet regulator] ordered them not to publish my articles." The Cyberspace Administration of China did not respond to a request for comment.

Zhao Sile, a mainland-based freelance journalist for Hong Kong publications, said the process of Chinese mainstream media outlets closing their doors to her has been gradual and quiet. "When I first started to write stories on human rights issues, I still had the opportunities to write for the Chinese mainstream media outlets on non-sensitive issues," Zhao said. "For example, for a while I wrote entertainment commentaries for *Beijing News*. Gradually, fewer and fewer people in the media circle would reach out to me about writing for them. No one told me to my face that they didn't want to keep in touch with me because of the human rights stories I wrote, but I'm sure I lost career opportunities and networks because of that." Zhao said she does not know whether those who chose not to contact her were under direct government pressure or did so voluntarily for fear of government reprisal.

Ye Du said the Social Credit System would further restrict activities of dissident writers like him. "When information about everyone and everything is online and connected, it would be much easier for the Chinese government to locate, surveil and control us," he said.

Zhao Sile said the credit system would have a chilling effect even on mainstream journalists who are critical of the government in private and occasionally express such opinions online but hold back for fear of retaliation. "The Social Credit System is to make sure the government's 'enemies'—those whose opinions do not align with the government—have nowhere to hide," Zhao said. "You already see how people can withdraw from expressing critical opinions online because they are afraid that their accounts can be shut down. If the government can enforce real-name registration and closely link people's speech to their daily life and economic opportunities, it will be an extremely powerful tool to force people into self-censorship."

Other journalists, however, say they doubt the credit system will be put in place on the scale that is currently envisioned. Gu Xi, a former editor for the news website NetEase, said the Chinese government's primary source of legitimacy is China's economic growth, and it would not want to restrict business activities. "Lowering your credit score [due to your online writing] and then restricting your ability to buy or sell stuff online do no good to the Chinese government. The government collects taxes from business transactions. The economy is what worries the Chinese government the most, not the people who badmouth the government," Gu said.

Liu Hu also expressed doubts about how much citizens will buy into the government's credit score rating. "The Chinese government has increasingly targeted online rumor-mongering, but more and more people have come to the realization that the government is the bigger rumormonger, and to crack down on rumor-mongering is to suppress people from speaking the truth," he said.

If Liu is right, the prospective buyer of that secondhand bike might simply ignore the journalist's credit score due to their lack of faith in the government's rating system. Whether other individuals, institutions and agencies that rely on credit scores would do the same remains to be seen.

Yaqiu Wang is Asia research associate for the Committee to Protect Journalists. She has a master of arts in International Affairs from George Washington University. Wang's articles on civil society and human rights in China have appeared in Foreign Policy, The Atlantic, China Change *and elsewhere.*

8. Chinese Import

By Emily Parker

Russian Prime Minister Dmitry Medvedev uses a smartphone at the Aquatics World Championships in Kazan, Russia, in August 2015. Moscow is trying to bring the internet under its control.

(Reuters/Hannibal Hanschke)

Russia has embarked on an ambitious social experiment. Just a few years ago, Russians had a mostly free internet. Now Moscow is looking toward Beijing, trying to imitate the Chinese model of internet control. Yet the Kremlin will likely find that once you give people internet freedom, it isn't so easy to completely take it away.

I lived in Moscow in 2010, after spending years researching internet activism in China. I quickly found that Russia and China had very different attitudes toward the web. China had countless human censors and automatic keyword filters, as well as a firewall that blocked great quantities of "sensitive" content. In Russia, by contrast, you could find almost any information online. Authorities didn't make a strong effort to censor the internet because the internet wasn't a political threat.

This all changed in late 2011 and early 2012, when Moscow was the site of the largest anti-government protests since the end of the Soviet Union. Social media played a significant role in organizing those protests, and Russian President Vladimir Putin took note. A flurry of new rules sprouted up, including a law that granted Russian authorities the power to block online content.

The Kremlin will see that China is a tough act to follow. Because, let's face it, Beijing has done a pretty good job of allowing internet access on its own terms. China has some 700 million people online as well as great restrictions on the flow of information. The Great Firewall of China has blocked overseas sites such as Twitter, Facebook and YouTube and media including *The New York Times* and *The Wall Street Journal*. Human censors, often working at Chinese tech companies, monitor and edit online conversations.

Russian authorities seem to admire this approach. In 2016, former Chinese internet czar Lu Wei and Great Firewall architect Fang Binxing visited Moscow to meet with a group called the Safe Internet League. In early November 2016, a Russian court upheld a decision to block LinkedIn, sounding a warning to foreign internet firms that operate in the country. Russian law requires websites that store the personal data of Russian citizens to do so on Russian servers. Google, Twitter and Facebook all risk being blocked in Russia if they refuse to store such personal data on Russian soil.

Both Russia and China have made clear that they wish to regulate the internet as they see fit. Chinese President Xi Jinping has stressed the importance of internet sovereignty, which basically means that individual countries should have the right to choose their own model of cyber governance. In this context, "sovereign" can be roughly translated into "free from U.S. interference." Putin has taken this idea one step further by calling the internet a "CIA project." By this logic, Russia needs to proactively protect its own interests in the information sphere, whether by cracking down on online dissent or using the internet to spread its own version of events. It remains to be seen if and how Trump's relationship with Putin will affect the Kremlin's approach to internet governance.

Russia internet expert Andrei Soldatov, author of the book *The Red Web*, says the Kremlin "certainly looks for something close to the China approach these days, mostly because many other things failed—filtering is porous, global platforms defy local legislation and are still available." Soldatov says that Moscow would like to put "critical infrastructure" under direct government control, such as the national system of domain distribution, internet exchange points and cables that cross borders. But this approach, which may not be successful, is more of an emergency measure than a realistic attempt to regulate the internet on a day-to-day basis.

It is probably too late to cut Russia off from the World Wide Web. China, on the other hand, recognized early on that the internet was both an opportunity and a threat. Beijing wanted to enjoy the economic gains of connectivity without sacrificing political control. "The Russian internet is very well connected and very competitive," explains Leonid Volkov, opposition politician and founder of Russia's Internet Protection Society. "The Chinese internet developed itself as a very closed structure from the very beginning; the Runet didn't."

China's isolated internet culture has given rise to formidable domestic companies. It was once easy to dismiss China's local tech players as mere "copycats"—Sina Weibo imitating Twitter, Baidu imitating Google and so on. But now, some of these companies, notably Tencent's WeChat, have become so powerful that we may soon see Western companies imitating them. Chinese domestic players have become so successful that many internet users aren't longing for their Western competitors.

One could argue that these companies' prowess is largely due to the fact that Facebook and Twitter were blocked and Google dramatically exited the country, citing concerns about censorship and cybersecurity. In Russia, on the other hand, U.S. tech companies like Google have made significant traction. Facebook may not be as popular as the Russian social network VKontakte (VK), but the American platform has a devoted following, especially among political activists. "The Facebook audience is much smaller than VK's," Volkov says. But he adds that those users make up "the whole cultural, scientific, political elite. In my opinion, the decision-makers in Kremlin do clearly realize: The potential harm of blocking the Facebook is higher than the potential benefit."

Soldatov agrees. "VK is popular among a completely different audience. The Facebook audience is much more loyal to the platform; it's mostly urban advanced intelligentsia. They learned to use Facebook shortly before or during the protests in Moscow, and they won't give it up because of the pressure—they use Facebook as the place for debate, not to share cats."

This raises a larger question: How can a government deprive citizens of an internet freedom that they once enjoyed? There are at least some signs that Russian internet users will put up a fight. A Russian petition in protest of antiterror laws that would threaten internet freedom reached more than 100,000 signatures in just a little over a month. Russians also came out to protest, sending the message that "the internet belongs to us."

Not even China can completely control the internet. Those who are determined to find information can find a tool, say, a virtual private network, to jump over the firewall. China has been home to a relatively small but energetic Twitter population, for example, despite the fact that the service is blocked. Russian censors will face the same challenge. In recent years, there has been an ongoing increase in Russian use of Tor, a browser that can be used to circumvent censorship. As a Global Voices article noted, "the increase in censorship closely mirrors the upward trend in interest towards Tor."

While the Russian government uses the internet and other media to spread its own propaganda, Putin also understands that technology can be a weapon of the opposition. The internet on its own will not cause a revolution in Russia, but if a revolutionary moment arose, technology would be a powerful tool for organization. Beijing figured this out a long time ago, and now the Kremlin understands it too.

Emily Parker *is the author of the nonfiction book* Now I Know Who My Comrades Are *about internet activism in China, Cuba and Russia, and is a former staff reporter for* The Wall Street Journal *and* The New York Times.

9. Willing Accomplice

By Andrew Finkel

Can Dündar, then editor-in-chief of *Cumhuriyet*, center left, and Ankara bureau chief Erdem Gül greet supporters as they arrive for a court hearing in Istanbul in March 2016.

(Reuters/Osman Orsal)

Turkey's bloody, failed military coup on July 15, 2016, and the ruthless crackdown that followed are testament to the country's escalating crisis of democracy. Though the crisis had been developing for years, with journalists and independent media outlets facing intense legal pressures from a government intent on serving elite interests rather than a free and open society, recent events illustrate a grave, new peril: the compliance and even complicity of the nation's mainstream media in its own emasculation and the suppression of objective news coverage.

My own experience as a journalist in both the Turkish language and the international press for more than 25 years has convinced me of both the importance and the insufficiency of "naming and shaming" the state's authoritarian tactics. After having stood trial in a Turkish court for writing columns that the government disliked, I realized it is necessary to acknowledge corruption within the nation's media organizations, including those that knowingly publish propaganda or decline to report—or to fully and objectively report—news that the government does not condone.

Despite the pervasiveness of social media, Turkey's strong governing party now controls the public discourse like never before by systematically exerting control over privately owned media and crowding out a more pluralistic press. Previous Turkish governments often defied international media standards; yet, the current regime does so with impunity and within its own definition of democratic norms. At issue for journalists is not only how the media should respond to these repressive tactics but how it should address problems within its own ranks.

My first confrontation with Turkish authorities occurred in 1999 over columns published in a Turkish-language newspaper that were critical of the army's conduct in the Kurdish majority regions. The prosecutor claimed the columns demeaned the country's military, an offense that at the time carried a potential six years imprisonment.

In response, the Committee to Protect Journalists wrote a public letter of protest on my behalf to the Turkish prime minister. But with the ingratitude to which journalists are all too prone, I went on to use CPJ's own website to criticize what I believed to be the organization's inherently blinkered approach—something I believed CPJ shared with other press freedom watchdogs.

I was thankful to have my case publicized but felt that Turkish journalists would remain at risk as long as one of the deeply rooted causes of their mistreatment remained unaddressed: the corruption and collusion of the media itself. My own newspaper, which had fired me months before under what I later learned were the express orders of the military-led National Security Council, did not even report on the trial or many others like it. The poorly kept secret of those working in the Turkish press was that journalists needed as much protection from their own newspapers as they did from the courts.

Since then, conditions have worsened considerably—in the severity of the government's tactics and in the collusion of the mainstream media. To put the current situation in context, in early 1999 there were 27 journalists in Turkish prisons, earning Ankara the infamous title it has claimed on many occasions since, as the world's foremost jailer of journalists.

During that era of unstable coalition governments, increasingly powerful media organizations played the roles of kingmakers. Press barons bartered their support for privatization tenders, for lucrative changes in land zoning, for government-affiliated advertising revenues and, most profitably of all during a decade of chronic inflation, for banking licenses. To retain leverage over politicians, newspapers still maintained a critical, non-sycophantic edge—one could not peddle influence, after all, without first having the muscle and influence to peddle. Many, however, were all too happy to plant stories at the request of national intelligence, to restrict coverage of the often-dirty war against Kurdish separatists in the country's southeast or to acquiesce in the dismissal of senior columnists and correspondents.

That dynamic has become far more pronounced in the years since. As of this writing, close to 146 Turkish journalists are behind bars— a more than fourfold increase since 1999, according to figures compiled by the independent journalist platform P24; the figures include 33 journalists who were in prison before the July 15 coup. Many other journalists have fled abroad, and, in some cases, the spouses and relatives they left behind have been denied passports. Other organizations have reached slightly different totals (CPJ, in its most recent prison census, was able to confirm at least 81 journalists had been jailed in relation to their work). Despite the difficulty of precisely quantifying the numbers, this much is clear: Turkey is the foremost jailer of journalists, with more journalists under lock-and-key than habitual offenders China, Iran and Egypt combined.

Many of the detentions and arrests followed the July 15 coup attempt and the subsequent imposition of a national state of emergency, which allowed authorities to suspend habeas corpus and adherence to the European Convention on Human Rights for 30 days.

At first glance, this crackdown might appear to be an attempt, however blunt, to punish anyone associated with Fethullah Gülen, an exiled cleric and founder of what is known as the Gülen (or Hizmet, which translates to "service") Movement, which the government accuses of having engineered the putsch.

Journalists were not the only ones to suffer in the wake of the failed coup. Reuters reported that three months later, more than 32,000 people were still under arrest (by December 2016, Reuters reported the number was up to 41,000), and more than 100,000 state employees had lost their jobs. There has been a wholesale purge of the judiciary, the universities and schools, the army, the police, the national intelligence and the rest of the civil service. Businesses have been seized and even hospitals closed.

The criteria for imposing these measures are not transparent, and the modus operandi of the purge has been capricious. Having a credit card at Bank Asya—a Gülen-associated finance house—or subscribing to the Gülenist flagship newspaper *Zaman* have been grounds for dismissal and even police detention.

In this environment, it is no longer possible to simply blame independent news organizations for hanging their staff out to dry because 46 newspapers, 29 TV channels, three news agencies, 31 radio stations, 16 magazines and 28 publishing houses have themselves been shut down in the aftermath of the failed coup, according to P24, based on open sources. Most of the organizations affected were outside the mainstream, including Zarok TV, a children's cartoon channel broadcast in Kurdish. Thousands working in the media have lost their jobs. With mainstream media under its firm control, the government has found it relatively easy to pick off the "independent" stragglers.

Open war against the Gülen movement predates the attempted coup, back to December 2013, when police and prosecutors accused senior government figures and their families of high-level corruption. At that time, the government described the police raids that accompanied these accusations as an attempted coup—the work of Gülenist sympathizers within the ranks of the bureaucracy trying to establish a parallel state. *Zaman,* once Turkey's largest-circulating daily, as well as a former firm supporter of the government, was placed under court-appointed administrators in March 2016 and then transformed into a pro-government newspaper before publication ceased at the end of the following July. Other Gülenist-linked publications and broadcasting organizations suffered similar fates. The government went on to adopt a practice initiated by the military of denying access to press conferences for publications of which it did not approve—notably those affiliated with the Gülen movement.

This practice accelerated after the coup. As CPJ reported in August 2016, Turkey's General Directorate for Press, Broadcasting and Information—the bureau within the prime minister's office responsible for accrediting journalists—revoked the credentials of 115 journalists whom it alleges were associated with Gülen.

However intricate the Gülenist involvement in the July 15 attempted coup proves to be, any legitimately elected government has both the right and the obligation to defend itself from a military takeover. Had the coup succeeded or had skirmishes between troops and government supporters been more protracted, the death toll would likely have been far greater. Some 240 people died in the hours after the coup—of whom roughly 157 were civilians, including one journalist for a pro-government newspaper.

In the weeks after the declaration of the state of emergency, however, it became apparent that the authorities cast their dragnet far wider than those associated with Gülenist media. Many who happened to work for these outlets cannot credibly be accused of supporting a coup d'état or even to have had Gülenist sympathies. Kurdish publications are generally antithetical to Gülen; yet, police detained 28 journalists after a raid on the *Azadiya Welat,* while another pro-Kurdish paper, *Özgür Gündem,* was closed down with cases initiated against a series of prominent journalists and writers who attempted to show solidarity by acting as "honorary editors" for the day. Two journalists from the left-wing *Evrensel* newspaper were also detained, though they were released after 16 days.

In its 2014 annual report, Freedom House flagged this wave of arrests and closures as an acceleration of an existing trend to choke off dissent. The report also relegated the Turkish press from the status of "partly free" to "not free."

The Freedom House decision to demote Turkey's status was based in part on the wholesale dismissal of journalists in the wake of the 2013 Gezi Park demonstrations, which, at the time, the government also described as an attempted coup. A huge catalog of anecdotal evidence, particularly from telephone conversations leaked onto the internet in early 2014, illustrate government efforts to micromanage reporting of the private media groups beholden to it. Then–Prime Minister Tayyip Erdoğan was overheard in leaked recordings reducing the proprietor of one newspaper group to tears while forcing him to fire a leading columnist. Erdoğan also demanded that a TV station alter the ticker at the bottom of the screen for giving too much attention to the leader of an opposition party. Since Gezi, it has become increasingly common for six or more pro-government papers to go to press with the exact same headline.

The question I raised nearly two decades ago was why the Turkish public would rise to the defense of newspapers that seemed indifferent even to the injustices committed against its own journalists. At the time, it was hard to find an interlocutor for the world's sense of outrage. The then–prime minister, Bülent Ecevit, was himself a journalist who openly suggested that his coalition government lacked the power to grapple with an authoritarian structure that was deeply embedded within the state.

That is why the increasing corruption of the mainstream media is so crucial—it has become a willing accomplice to this new authoritarianism. That, too, is an escalation rooted in a long-standing problem. In 1997, the military successfully engineered a change in government in what is often referred to as a postmodern coup. One of its principal tools was to engage media owners and senior editors who publicly pledged their services to the military-led National Security Council to unseat a coalition led by the pro-Islamic Welfare Party. Journalists critical of that collaboration were fired. The subsequent court closure of the Welfare Party was directly responsible for the formation and ascendency of the now-governing Justice and Development Party (AKP). The media's role in this "coup" left a bitter residue and inspired the AKP when it came to power to create a national media firmly under its own control.

The parent companies of media organizations in the 1990s were increasingly invested in banking and financial service. Media benefited from and helped to oil the vicious circle in which the government paid ever-higher interest rates to roll over its debts. Twin interest rate and currency rate crises in 2000 and 2001 led to the collapse of all but one of the media-owned banks and the seizure of their newspaper and television stations to pay back their debts. The financial cost of this crisis—about a third of Turkey's gross domestic product (GDP)—led to the obliteration of a whole postwar generation of politicians and shoehorned the AKP into power in 2002. Media assets in public receivership were subsequently sold to corporations that had cultivated connections to the new regime.

The current pattern of media proprietorship is not, however, simply a case of history repeating itself. Previously, media owners used their power to gain entry into non-media business. Today, contractors, shopping mall owners and healthcare or energy magnates view press ownership as a sort of levy for doing business with the government. Some pay this tribute reluctantly and after bitter complaint. The result is that the great bulk of the Turkish media is under the control of proprietors who have no interest in holding government up to scrutiny. Far from speaking truth to power, editorial control is willingly surrendered to political superiors. Erdoğan admitted on the record that the proprietor of *Milliyet* newspaper consulted with him over whom to appoint as its editor-in-chief. One of the few large media corporations to make the transition into the AKP era, the Doğan group, did so only after being declawed by its parent company, which faced a tax fine approximately equal to its entire market capital. Many Doğan employees privately confessed to me that self-censorship is now the rule, not the exception. There have been recent meetings in which the president and senior ministers met with owners, editors and senior columnists of the pro-government media. These private discussions of media coverage are publicly acknowledged and described unabashedly as "closed to the press."

Independent media in Turkey finds itself with both hands tied behind its back. In addition to facing political and judicial harassment, it is subject to unfair competition from rivals that view media ownership as a public relations expense, not a for-profit concern. And this occurs in a digital age in which selling news content is itself a growing financial challenge. There is no incentive for press groups to forsake a business model that works, even if through corruption, for the icy waters of genuine competition.

Media outlets often give no—or, at best, scant—market value to integrity or reputation. Much of the pro-government Turkish press now falls into the category of propaganda. Polemical headlines accompany Photoshopped realities. To cite one particularly ludicrous example, the iconic Henry Ries photo of the Berlin airlift was used to illustrate an article on how the U.S. supports coups in Guatemala and throughout the world. Similarly, a *Christian Science Monitor* reporter who happened to share the same name as a man convicted of murdering his pregnant wife in California was paraded on the front pages as a "hired assassin" brought from the United States to Turkey to assist in the coup.

If all this seems harmlessly absurd, it cannot be dismissed as such. Crude fabrications come at the expense of the kind of professional reporting that would answer citizens' concerns over what truly transpired the night of July 15, 2016. A headline writer's desire to extract revenge or to deflect attention from the government's responsibility for failing to anticipate the coup undermines objective investigation of the consequences of the purge for key institutions and businesses. Rather than display solidarity on issues of press freedom, pro-government columnists see as part of their function accusing other journalists of treason with Stalinesque zeal and calling on public prosecutors to do their worst.

This grim situation raises many questions, perhaps the most interesting of which is difficult to adequately answer: why a government that enjoys a high level of popular support still seeks to repress opposition media. Among the surfeit of possible explanations is that the government sees power as a zero-sum game and that to lose even a bit of control (as when it briefly lost its parliamentary majority in the June 2016 general election) would cause the whole edifice of its authority to crumble. Another is that the government is a victim of a sort of "Midas touch" phenomenon, whereby it controls the media at the expense of that media's ability to convey credible information.

In many cases, government officials may not actually believe their own propaganda, but they understand how fickle public opinion can be, hence the regime's great concern over the effects of social media and the almost systematic way in which access to Twitter or Facebook is denied whenever serious news—such as bombings or coup attempts—occurs. Erdoğan once declared Twitter the greatest social evil, presumably because it is not easy to control.

Though it seems risible that the AKP's leader would define the Gezi Park environmental protest as a coup, in retrospect, that anxiety might have been real. Even the paranoid sometimes have actual enemies, as illustrated by the attempts of putschists to seize the television stations on the night of July 15, 2016. The great irony of the coup attempt was that while the president's foes stuck to the antediluvian rulebook and seized the state broadcaster TRT, he rallied his supporters with an interview on FaceTime, with the CNN Turk anchor holding her iPhone up to the camera.

At a time when journalists are being dragged to police stations under the emergency rule regulation, it might seem precious to continue emphasizing the danger that the degradation of news and the contraction of the public realm represents. I understood all too well the difficulties an organization such as CPJ (which is engaged in the heavy lifting to keep journalists safe from their own governments) faces when attempting to turn around the guns to target media organizations for supporting undemocratic practices. It is already a tricky endeavor to define a "real journalist" worthy of protection. Devising a strategy to name and shame those who abuse journalism to threaten others, or defining who is doing "real news," is to pry open a Pandora's box.

At the same time, it is clear from the worsening situation of the Turkish press that the mainstream strategy of private advocacy and public indignation has failed to produce results. A tentative step was a Freedom House report that signposted the erosion of democracy in

Turkey after 2013 by analyzing corruption within media itself. But as a first principle, one point needs to be made widely: It is impossible to fully protect journalists when the core tenets of journalism are themselves in peril.

Andrew Finkel is an Istanbul-based correspondent, a founder of P24 (Punto24, an association to defend independent journalism in Turkey) and author of Turkey: What Everyone Needs to Know.

10. Edited by Drug Lords

By Elisabeth Malkin

The entrance to *Noroeste* is covered with bullet holes after gunmen opened fire on the newspaper's regional office in the Pacific resort city of Mazatlán, Mexico, on September 1, 2010.

(AP/Christiann Davis)

Adrián López Ortiz, the general director of Grupo Noroeste, a media group that owns the newspaper *Noroeste* in the northwestern Mexican city of Culiacán, was driving home from the airport in April 2014 when an SUV intercepted him. Two armed men got out and grabbed him, and he feared that he was going to be kidnapped. But they had other plans. One of them drove off in his car and the other stayed behind, kicked López and then shot him in both legs.

What followed was a variation on what has become the theme of many attacks on the Mexican media.

Two young men were quickly arrested and charged with aggravated auto theft. The governor of the state of Sinaloa described the crime as "bad luck" and congratulated the authorities for their quick work. Case closed.

López is not convinced. "There is no evidence to say that it came from the government," he said. "But I have elements to say that it wasn't a common crime." To begin with, he said, "The modus operandi didn't fit." He had been followed from the airport, and his stolen car was recovered within three hours. And he was shot while he was down, when he no longer posed a threat to the assailants. Later, when he asked to review the footage from official security cameras, the authorities refused. "There are many inconsistencies," he said.

In September 2016, a judge released one of two suspects, citing insufficient evidence and a violation of due process.

The assault on López followed a string of attacks on *Noroeste*, which has long had a reputation for independence in Sinaloa, the home state of some of Mexico's most powerful drug lords.

Among the attacks, the motorcycles the newspaper's deliverymen used were stolen. Its photographers were beaten by police when they covered a march by supporters of the jailed drug kingpin known as "El Chapo," or Joaquín Guzmán Loera. Armed men attacked the lobby of the newspaper's building, and an armed group burst into the home of its sales director and stole his cell phones and laptop.

Threats came over the phone and the internet, and the newspaper's website was hacked. López estimates that the newspaper has filed some 100 complaints with the Sinaloa state prosecutor over the attacks, and yet there remains "100 percent impunity."

That impunity is the common thread running through many of the efforts to censor the media in Mexico. Whether the source of the attacks is organized crime or the government, or some combination of the two, the purpose is always the same: to intimidate and silence journalists. "Killing journalists is free in Mexico," López said. The formal structure to investigate the crime exists, he added, but it is merely a simulation.

Mexico's National Human Rights Commission said in November 2016 that 119 journalists have been killed since the beginning of 2000, and 20 more disappeared between 2005 and 2015. There have been 50 attacks on newsrooms in the past decade. In 90 percent of the cases, the crimes have gone unpunished, the commission said. The threat is strongest against independent media in Mexico's provinces, where a number of independent family-owned newspapers must play a careful balancing act as they seek to cover the news in a way that holds government to account.

Those newspapers were among the most important players in the more assertive media that contributed to Mexico's long democratic transition, according to Javier Garza, the former editor of *El Siglo de Torreón*. That transition seemed complete with the election in 2000 of a president from an opposition party after more than seven decades of rule by the Institutional Revolutionary Party, known as the PRI. But Mexican politics have also become messier. Freed from the old structures of one-party rule, governors became all-powerful, regardless of whether they were from the PRI or the opposition.

At the same time, conflicts among drug trafficking organizations grew more violent as the federal government cracked down. State and local governments often sat on the sidelines and organized crime burrowed its way into power, buying, co-opting and threatening officials and the police.

"If the government is infiltrated by organized crime, then you have whole networks of complicity," said Mariclaire Acosta, a human rights activist and the director of Freedom House in Mexico. "Everything has to do with the action or the omission of the authorities."

The nexus between organized crime and the authorities means that any effort to silence newspapers by one actor may work to the benefit of others. If a newspaper stops covering drug trafficking violence, for example, the silence removes one source of pressure for the local government to stop the attacks. If the government dismisses an attack on a journalist as a common crime, it sends a message to the gangs that they are free to act.

"The government and the crime groups benefit from each other," said Daniel Rosas, a longtime reporter for and editor of the online edition of *El Mañana*, a newspaper in the city of Nuevo Laredo, on the border with Texas. "There is a symbiosis." *El Mañana* is on the front lines of the drug war; editor Roberto Mora was murdered in 2004 after he criticized the government's inaction in the face of drug gangs that were beginning to take over communities.

The murder sent an unmistakable message that organized crime would not tolerate certain kinds of coverage. Two years later, an armed group burst into the newsroom, shot at the staff and threw a fragmentation grenade, leaving one reporter paralyzed.

In 2012, armed men threw a grenade and shot at the façade of *El Mañana*'s building, though no one was hurt. Like *Noroeste*, *El Mañana* has suffered other attacks as well, including on its motorcycle deliverymen and on its internet servers. Sometimes, reporters and editors get messages in advance warning them not to publish a particular story.

The violence—and the authorities' failure to investigate and prosecute it—forced the newspaper to make a difficult choice: *El Mañana* no longer publishes stories about organized crime in Nuevo Laredo.

"There is no rule of law to guarantee that I will be protected for what I tell you," said Ninfa Cantú, *El Mañana*'s publisher and the granddaughter of the newspaper's founder.

The silence can seem puzzling to readers. "It's absurd not to publish what everybody knows is happening, what's on social media," Rosas said.

It seems even stranger because *El Mañana* does cover drug violence in the rest of its state, Tamaulipas, and across Mexico. At the same time, other Tamaulipas media cover violence in Nuevo Laredo, including the newspapers that are also called *El Mañana* in the border cities of Reynosa and Matamoros to the east. They were founded by Cantú's grandfather but broke away decades ago.

All of this information is available online, which makes it even harder to understand why the local drug gang in Nuevo Laredo is so concerned with what the local newspapers print.

"It's more a situation of control," Rosas said. "When we have our editorial meetings, we ask what we can write about and what we can't write about."

But if *El Mañana* cannot write directly about violence in Nuevo Laredo, its journalists have found many other ways to cover the story of their city.

The newspaper has not shied away from covering official corruption and was very critical of the past state governor for his failure to fight organized crime. It has reported on the cases of two previous state governors who have been indicted in the United States on drug charges.

What also matters to readers is the effect of violence on investment in the city, which is a major border crossing hub and an assembly manufacturing center. Rosas has begun a new investigative team that will take on issues such as pollution and track the activities of legislators.

"The only thing we cannot write about is violence and local drug trafficking," said Mauricio Flores, the newspaper's adjunct director.

The connection between local government and organized crime in Tamaulipas leads to a long list of subjects that are "hands off" for reporters in the state, said Garza, including drug trafficking. That includes migrant smuggling and corruption among migration authorities, the customs agency and prostitution and extortion in local nightclubs.

At *Noroeste* in Sinaloa, the threats have not stopped the newspaper from covering drug trafficking, but it has taken a more careful approach, including keeping violence off the front pages unless the news is part of a larger context. "*Noroeste* cannot be part of narco communication," López said.

And it continues to publish investigative stories, like its coverage of the torture of suspects by police, the planned construction of a fertilizer plant on protected wetlands by a former governor and the opacity surrounding lucrative construction bids for two hospitals.

"There are conditions to practice good journalism," López said. But he added, "Our journalism has to criticize with very precise investigations." Many of those reports are reproduced by the national press, and the visibility provides a measure of protection for the newspaper.

Noroeste has also focused its coverage on other issues—such as entrepreneurship or soft news—that matter to readers in Sinaloa, which has a vibrant business community and a strong sense of community centered around sports, music and food.

The high-quality journalism of both newspapers ensures loyal readerships, strong circulation and steady advertising. That, in turn, provides a commercial buffer at a time when Mexican newspapers, like newspapers everywhere, face the challenge of making up for declining print advertising.

Economic stress means that many newspapers—and broadcast media—are easy prey for another kind of censorship, the effort by the government to simply buy the media off by pouring money into advertising. Research by Fundar, a government watchdog group in Mexico City, and international free expression group Article 19 has documented the spending of the equivalent of hundreds of millions of U.S. dollars for advertising each year by the federal and state governments—a form of "soft censorship" that involves pouring money into dozens of newspapers in the provinces that seem to exist merely to run thinly disguised press releases recounting the actions of officials as they supervise handouts in poor neighborhoods or open public works projects.

Official advertising can account for up to 30 percent of ad revenue for national media and 80 percent for regional newspapers and broadcasters, said Ana Cristina Ruelas, the director of Article 19 for Mexico and Central America. "The amount is overwhelming," she said. But politicians behave as though "it is cheaper to buy off the media than practice good government," she added.

Amid declining advertising revenue, government revenue becomes even more important for newspapers. But both *Noroeste* and *El Mañana* can afford to do with little or no government advertising. At the federal level, this flow of advertising has increased under the presidency of Enrique Peña Nieto, who returned the PRI to power in 2012. Although the national media was less acquiescent than local outlets, coverage of the federal government was more muffled than it had been under the earlier opposition governments. That changed in 2014, after an investigative team working with the broadcast journalist Carmen Aristegui revealed that Peña Nieto's wife had bought a luxury mansion on favorable terms from a government contractor. The news contributed to a collapse in the president's popularity.

Aristegui was fired by her employer, MVS Communications, four months later over a whistleblowing website she helped set up. MVS said she used the company's name without its permission, but many saw her firing as retribution for her investigation. Despite the high ratings and visibility she could bring, no other broadcaster has hired her (although she continues with an interview show on CNN en Español and writes a column for the Mexico City daily *Reforma*). MVS owner Joaquín Vargas filed a lawsuit against Aristegui in May 2016, accusing her of "moral damage" for suggesting in a prologue she wrote for a book about the investigation that he had caved in to government pressure when he fired her.

Other public figures are beginning to use "moral damage" lawsuits to try to stifle coverage. Humberto Moreira, a former governor who multiplied the debt of the state of Coahuila by 100 times, is suing the newspaper *Vanguardia* and reporter Roxana Romero for documenting that he was receiving a teacher's pension without meeting the requirements for it.

The paper, which is based in the Coahuila state capital of Saltillo, was also subject to a denial-of-service cyberattack on its servers, and Romero was followed home one night, according to a *Vanguardia* editorial.

Moreira has filed two more lawsuits against a well-known radio host, Pedro Ferriz de Con, and a prominent human rights activist and columnist, Sergio Aguayo.

For every visible case, though, there are many more subtle forms of censorship that throw up constant hurdles to reporters. Mayors or governors call owners asking to delay or halt a story. "A publisher has to make a decision," Garza said. "It's done discreetly, it's done very quietly." Many reporters are paid by the story and cannot afford to see an article spiked, which pushes them to cover news that does not challenge anyone, like official events. Andrés Resillas, who runs a website in the state of Michoacán, faces down all these threats on his own.

He begins by rejecting government advertising that comes with strings attached. When he does an investigation and asks for the government's version, he said, "they always raise the issue of advertising and I tell them, if you want to take it away, then go ahead." Instead, he works other jobs to help support his site, *Revista Búsqueda*, including giving courses to journalists.

There is another cost to his independence: His site has been hacked four times in the last 18 months, perhaps a response to his reports on corruption at the state electoral authority. "Digital security is where we have to put a lot of emphasis because it's where we are vulnerable," he said. An electoral official threatened to sue, and Resillas posted all the supporting documents for his investigation on his Facebook page in defense.

Michoacán is a center for organized crime and there, too, Resillas has been forced to tread carefully. For a year, he did not publish anything about drug trafficking. Now, he reproduces stories about organized crime and local resistance in the state that are published by the national newspaper *Reforma,* even though local newspapers remain silent.

There might be a risk in giving visibility to the issues on his site. "It's like stretching a rubber band and when you see it's going to snap, you loosen it a bit," he said.

He might as well have been describing the tension that pulls at many Mexican reporters and the response they must gauge every day.

Elisabeth Malkin is a reporter for The New York Times in Mexico City and has lived in Mexico since 1992.

11. Self-Restraint vs. Self-Censorship

By Jean-Paul Marthoz

A French police officer uses a sniffer dog to check a stadium in Nice in February 2016. European cities have stepped up security measures after a series of terror attacks.

(Reuters/Eric Gaillard)

Europen journalists are on edge. Since the brutal execution of eight colleagues at the French satirical weekly *Charlie Hebdo* on January 7, 2015, they have become acutely aware that they are in the firing line of extremists.

"Journalists will not cede to fear," said Ricardo Gutierrez, the European Federation of Journalists' general secretary, after a second attack, on November 13, 2015, claimed the life of another journalist who was covering the Eagles of Death Metal concert at the Bataclan Theater.

Most vowed not to submit to such fears, though some (cartoonists, in particular) confessed at the time that they thought twice before filing a story or writing a column that might trigger the ire of terrorists.

Their unease also stems from a nagging feeling that authorities, despite their public commitment to defending free speech and a free press, look at journalists with a degree of suspicion, as if they are a hindrance in the fight against terrorism.

The question facing journalists in such an environment is: At what point does self-restraint become self-censorship?

European Union member states do not go as far as Turkey President Recep Tayyip Erdoğan, who rushes to denounce critical reporters and columnists as accomplices of terrorism. But former British Prime Minister Margaret Thatcher's characterization of the media as "the oxygen of terrorism" is treated as dogma by many in European security circles. By describing the situation as a "war," government officials expect the media to toe the line.

The risk was highlighted in a January 26, 2016, report by the Council of Europe's Committee on Political Affairs and Democracy, which noted that "combating terrorism and protecting Council of Europe standards (respect for human rights, rule of law and common values) are not contradictory but complementary. . . . While acknowledging the need for member States to have access to sufficient legal instruments to combat terrorism efficiently, the Assembly warns against the risk that counterterrorism measures may introduce disproportionate restrictions or sap democratic control and thus violate fundamental freedoms and the rule of law, in the name of safeguarding State security."

Little by little, drop by drop, the media integrate these concerns into their news routines and some even anticipate or go beyond security service orders or recommendations. Though they may reject any notion of self-censorship, "caution" has become the byword of "ethical" or "responsible" journalism.

After the killing of a Catholic priest on July 26, 2016, at Saint-Étienne-du-Rouvray in Normandy, the leading French news channel BFM TV decided to stop showing pictures of terrorists. "We want to avoid putting terrorists on the same level as their victims whose photos we do broadcast," said BFM TV news director Hervé Béroud. The 24-hour news channel banned in particular a photograph of one of the killers, "a smiling beautiful young kid who had just cut a priest's throat," Béroud added.

France's newspaper of record, *Le Monde*, took a similar approach. "Following the Nice attack (on July 14) we will no longer publish photos of killers in order to prevent potential effects of posthumous glorification. Other debates on our practices are going on," wrote its editor-in-chief, Jérôme Fenoglio. The decision was limited to photos taken by terrorists themselves or drawn from their daily life before they committed attacks. The ban did not include photos that had clear news value, *Le Monde* added.

Europe 1, one of the top French radio stations, went even further by deciding not to name the killers. "Such decision appears laudable, but it is unlikely that one of these terrorists was radicalized while reading *Le Monde*," Catholic University of Louvain professor of journalism ethics Benoit Grevisse said. "It ignores the reality of social media and internet sites. Besides, it contradicts a founding value of journalism ethics: the obligation to look for and publish the truth on matters of public interest. To make of non-publication an *a priori* implies that elements of information like names or faces would never be of public interest."

Although other newsrooms reaffirmed their right and perceived duty to show and name alleged terrorists, these initiatives reveal the ethical dilemmas the mainstream media faces in the coverage of terrorism. Appeals for restraint and responsibility have proliferated since the wave of attacks in France and Belgium, mainly because wall-to-wall coverage of these dramatic events led to a number of egregious mistakes and missteps. A few media outlets, and especially 24-hour news channels, crossed red lines in the wake of the *Charlie Hebdo* attack and during the hostage taking at the Hyper Cacher store in Paris a few days later. On February 12, 2015, the French audiovisual higher council, known as CSA, issued a strong statement highlighting 36 "failings" in the media's coverage of these events, in particular the broadcasting of information on the deployment of police forces that might have been watched by the terrorists, as well as the revelation that people were hiding in parts of the buildings where the terrorists were still active.

Likewise, in March 2016, a French newsweekly revealed that the Belgian police had found the DNA of Salah Abdeslam, a participant in the November 2015 attacks in Paris, and who was the most wanted fugitive in Europe, during a raid on a house in a Brussels suburb— a leak that could have tipped off Abdeslam. In another incident, the transmission truck of a major Belgian private TV channel was pre-positioned close to the house where Abdeslam was hiding before the police had even started its operations.

"They offer the security of my staff on the altar of ratings," the director of Belgium's judicial police, Claude Fontaine, said during a TV debate.

After each attack, media outlets have been slammed, including from inside the profession. On August 8, 2016, three weeks after the Nice slaughter, prize-winning columnist and writer Jean-Claude Guillebaud published a damning column titled, "When the Media Become Crazy."

There is no doubt that some in the media went into overdrive and lost sight of the rules of the ethical highway. But if the danger to journalistic integrity lies in overhyping terrorist acts, it also stems from the conviction some hold that the press should be part of the general fight against terrorism.

There is little doubt about where journalists stand. After Paris, Brussels and Nice, editorials, articles and broadcasts were universally filled with the strongest condemnation of these heinous acts. However, there is a danger that such concerns about potentially endangering public security or the desire to be in sync with a shocked public could lead journalists to defang their legitimate coverage of counterterrorism and minimize their watchdog role in the name of national unity or the common good.

A few Belgian journalists grumbled when on November 22, 2015, the Belgian police "invited" the press to go silent during a raid against suspected terrorist hideouts in Brussels, but the media complied and instead ran photos of cats on their websites until it was considered safe to report on the raids. "Are Belgian media more responsible or more servile than French ones?" asked *Le Monde*'s Brussels correspondent, Cécile Ducourtieux.

"Restricting the live coverage of police operations is considered legitimate, as long as they do not constitute an act of news censorship," said Jean-François Dumont, deputy general secretary of the Belgian Association of Professional Journalists.

Belgian journalists remained on the scene and continued filming without broadcasting live or posting online precise details on the location of the raids. But a few hours later they provided full coverage of the events.

"The media have a duty to monitor police actions; they have a duty of inventory," explained Jean-Pierre Jacqmin, the head of news for Belgium's Francophone public broadcaster RTBF.

In fact, they have of duty of going beyond "fusion journalism," which naturally prevails in the first hours following an attack and tends to be driven by empathy for the victims, calls for national unity, admiration for the rescue teams and respect for the security forces' mission.

The general consensus among journalists is that feelings of grief and humanity cannot supersede the press's duty to report the facts, including shocking or inconvenient facts. Some politicians are quick to stigmatize journalists who are out of step and insist on asking "Why?" at the risk of breaking the nation's emotional communion. During a November 26, 2015, Senate Q&A session, French Prime Minister Manuel Valls declared that he was "weary of those people always looking for excuses or cultural and sociological explanations" for the attacks. On January 9, 2016, in an homage to the victims of hostage murders at the Jewish store Hyper Cacher, Valls drove the point home. "Explaining is already a little bit like excusing," he said. His approach, however, was contradicted in a March 2016 report commissioned by the government after the November 2015 attacks. "Knowing the causes of a threat is the first condition to protect against it," wrote the authors, a team of researchers at the prestigious Athena Alliance (a collective of social sciences researchers), using words that also define the journalistic ethos.

The point is that revulsion over the attacks does not absolve journalists of their duty to tell the facts and ask tough questions. "On
the Opinion pages one factor taken into consideration was timing—
judging when readers would be willing to engage with an idea that
in the first 24 hours after the attacks may have jarred," *The Guardian's*
standards editor Chris Elliot wrote on November 23, 2015, just after
the Paris attacks. "The idea that these horrific attacks have causes and
that one of those causes may be the West's policies is something that
in the immediate aftermath might inspire anger. Three days later, it's a
point of view that should be heard."

Alain Genestar, the director of the glossy photojournalism magazine *Polka,* authored an editorial along those same lines in September
2016, defending the media's right and duty to inform independently.
"Every citizen is entitled to put in doubt the efficiency of the government's security policy when the death toll is of 230 dead in
18 months," he wrote. "Every citizen is entitled to ask explanations
from the Interior minister who, after the Nice attack, was tight-lipped.
Unity, in a true democracy, does not mean granting blind and deaf trust
to a man, even to the President." The headline of his editorial, "During
the attacks democracy continues," underlined that the response of
democratic states, the methods they use and their care not to enforce
abusive exemptions from the rule of law and fundamental rights are
crucial to the fight against terrorism. Few journalists, however, focus on
investigating stories that might question the effectiveness or the legality
of police and intelligence agencies' operations. Such issues are mostly
left to researchers of human rights or civil liberties associations.

"Some journalists may fear being shut off from inside sources
who provide them with tips on operations, arrests, or investigations,"
Andrew Stroehlein, European media director at Human Rights Watch,
said. "They may also be afraid of upsetting the public, who in times of
crisis tend to trust the authorities and consider maverick journalists as
unpatriotic or even as useful idiots of terrorism."

The idea expressed by former *Washington Post* publisher Katherine
Graham, that "news is the lifeblood of liberty," is not unanimously
shared. In the trade-off between liberty and security, most people,
according to many surveys, would choose a restriction of freedoms and
a security-first approach. In the wake of the July 14, 2016, "mad truck"

slaughter on the Promenade des Anglais in Nice, which killed at least 84 and wounded hundreds, an Institut Français d'Opinion Publique survey (IFOP) concluded that 81 percent of the French adult population agreed with the imposition of limits on the traditional liberal-democratic way of life to combat terrorism. "We are witnessing a form of democratic approval of a decline of democratic freedoms," said Paris University professor François Saint-Bonnet.

Some authorities may also be tempted to abuse the argument of public security or police safety to defend controversial policies unrelated to the terrorist threat. In August 2016, Christian Estrosi, a leading member of the opposition center-right party and a former mayor of Nice, threatened to sue social media users who shared photos of a team of municipal police questioning a modestly clad Muslim woman sitting on the beach. He claimed these photos, taken at the height of the controversy over the banning of the burkini, a full-body bathing suit, had led to threats against the agents.

Authorities are increasingly acting as if the threat of terrorism or public disorder could justify a number of exceptions to the freedom to report. In the Netherlands, the "public interest" or the risk to "public order" or "peaceful coexistence" was invoked to ban journalists from doing their most basic job when reporting on an issue of deep public interest: migration. In a number of Dutch small towns, the governments created a press ban to prevent journalists from covering public debates between the authorities and local residents over the opening of refugee centers. The authorities claimed the presence of cameras or reporters would inflame passions and derail efforts to discuss this controversial issue in a civil manner.

"In an open and democratic society, it is up to the media to decide what to report on, how to report and what methods to use," the Dutch Society of Editors in Chief complained.

But Sander Dekker, the Dutch State Secretary for Education, Culture and Science, supported the decision in an answer to a parliamentary question, arguing the measure was "not disproportionate."

Increasingly, democratic governments adopt public safety laws and measures that compromise the exercise of independent journalism. On June 30, 2015, the Spanish government put into force a Public Security Law, known as the gag law, which allows the imposition of heavy fines on anyone filming the police in action. Such laws, the Spanish government argued, are meant to protect the privacy and safety of security forces and their families. But human rights and press freedom groups complained that the law effectively undercuts the right of the press to monitor the behavior of the police and guarantees impunity for any abusive act or violation of fundamental rights.

In April 2016, Axier Lopez, a journalist working for the Basque magazine *Argia*, was the first journalist to be fined under the Spanish law. He had posted on his Twitter account an "unauthorized" photo of police making an arrest. "Through these images it is possible to identify the officers taking part in the operation, with the risk that for the officers can result from their public identification," the judge in the court case that followed said.

Likewise, in France, a "snooper's law" was put in force in July 2015, allowing the security services to intercept online conversations. The law does not exempt journalists and therefore poses a potential risk of intrusion in their legitimate work and compromises the confidentiality of sources, press freedom groups warned. The law "grants excessively large powers of very intrusive surveillance on the basis of broad and ill-defined aims, without prior judicial authorization and without an adequate and independent oversight mechanism," according to the U.N. Human Rights Committee.

Amid the debate over the media's—and, by extension, the public's—right to know, few question the idea that terrorism is a major threat to democratic societies. Most in the media are aware of its dangers and of their responsibility not to provide terrorists with the "oxygen of publicity." But terrorism is not only dangerous due to its violence against people who are often innocent civilians. It is also part of the killers' efforts to portray democracy as an empty shell that can easily be broken by fear. Terrorists attempt to chip away or even dismantle what constitutes the essential guarantees of an effective and vibrant democracy.

As a result, journalists who are attempting to be circumspect and cautious in their reporting must also address the reality that independent watchdog journalism is necessary, now more than ever, to protect democratic states and their citizens from their own instincts to overreact—essentially, that a free press can act as a guardrail against abuses and restrictions, which could effectively lead targeted countries into the terrorists' trap. Legendary rebel journalist I. F. Stone's assertion could serve as a warning. "All governments lie," Stone famously wrote in his 1967 book *In a Time of Torment*, "but disaster lies in wait for countries whose officials smoke the same hashish they give out."

As U.S. Senator J. William Fulbright advocated in an April 25, 1966, speech during the Vietnam War: "To criticize one's country is to do it a service and pay it a compliment. It is a service because it may spur the country to do better than it is doing; it is a compliment because it evidences a belief that the country can do better than it is doing. . . . Criticism, in short, is more than a right: it is an act of patriotism—a higher form of patriotism, I believe, than the familiar rituals of national adulation."

Jean-Paul Marthoz is a Belgian journalist and writer whose recent book on journalism and terrorism was published by UNESCO. He teaches global journalism at the Université Catholique de Louvain (Belgium) and is the Committee to Protect Journalists' former European Union representative.

12. Connecting Cuba

By Carlos Lauría

Cuban President Raúl Castro holds up a copy of the newspaper
Juventud Rebelde **in Havana in December 2010. Freedom of speech is**
still curbed despite a series of press reforms.

(AP/Ismael Francisco, Prensa Latina)

C uba's media landscape has begun opening up in recent years, transformed by a lively blogosphere, an increasing number of news websites carrying investigative reporting and news commentary and an innovative breed of independent reporters who are critical of, yet still support, socialist ideas.

The energized press scene contrasts with the island nation's restrictive legal framework, which curbs freedom of speech under the guise of protecting the "independence or territorial integrity of the state." Though the constitution bans private ownership of the press and all media are supposedly controlled by the one-party Communist state, the spread of independent reporting is a sign of change.

Reporters, from the most critical—who are known as dissidents—to journalism school graduates, documentary filmmakers and pro-revolutionary bloggers, are opening new spaces for free expression and entrepreneurial journalism that seemed off limits just a few years ago.

Bloggers said they have embraced the loosening of restrictions. "We are seeing opportunities that were inconceivable five years ago," said Alejandro Rodríguez, who quit his job in 2012 at *Adelante*, a state-run weekly in the eastern city of Camagüey, to start a blog.

However, many said that more work needs to be done, with the threat of arbitrary detention, vague and outdated laws and limitations on internet access slowing Cuba's press freedom progress.

Internet access in Cuba, which the U.N. rates among the lowest in the Western Hemisphere, is still inaccessible to most citizens. And though large-scale systematic state repression has eased significantly, the most strident opponents in the media say they still face harassment and intimidation from authorities.

The media field began expanding in 2011, when President Raúl Castro introduced market-style reforms to reinvent socialism, though many of those reforms have been implemented sluggishly and, in some cases, have been reversed.

When the call for loosening of restrictions was first made, the party leadership urged the Cuban population to be critical of the government and state institutions. Castro told the People's Assembly in a December 2010 speech not to fear discrepancies and differences of opinions.

Journalists, especially those working for the state press, have been emboldened by these statements. And though there is almost no criticism of government policies in the state media, most newspapers—including the national daily *Granma*—have started "Letters to the Editor" sections that provide a vehicle for Cubans to express opinions.

State journalists and academics in Havana said they recognize the need for the official press to become more critical, and some have called for a public information law. Laura Blanco Betancourt, a reporter for the state-owned provincial daily *Vanguardia*, acknowledged that the lack of "a culture of debate" had prevented candid discussions within the official press. José Ramón Vidal, a former editor of the daily *Juventud Rebelde*, went further in an interview published in the December 2015–March 2016 edition of Mexican magazine *Razón y Palabra*, where he argued that Cuba should change its "communication model" because "important social issues" were being left behind. Vidal, now a communications professor at the University of Havana, said the propaganda-based media model faced a crisis and that Cubans no longer paid attention to it.

Raudiel Peña Barrios, a lawyer in Havana, wrote in the online magazine *OnCuba*, "the mere fact that [freedom of information] is under discussion is big news in the Cuban context." In the article, "The Right to Information Cuba: Possibility or Utopia?," Peña said that such legislation "should help to democratize access to information."

Blanco Betancourt, who is based in Santa Clara province, said that a public communications strategy could help, adding that any such legislation "must include access to public information for all Cubans."

Though Cuba's tight grip on the press has waned in recent years, authorities still exert control over the media and the most critical independent journalists continue to face harassment. Long-term incarcerations have become rare since the 2003 crackdown (during which CPJ documented 29 journalists serving lengthy prison sentences), but detentions and summons are still common, CPJ research shows. The once-common tactic of accusing journalists of acting as "mercenaries" at the service of the United States has become almost obsolete.

The restoration of diplomatic ties between Washington and Havana in December 2014, coupled with then–U.S. President Barack Obama's historic March 2016 visit to Cuba, have made it harder for the government to justify press censorship as a means to protect the nation from American aggression, Cuban journalists said. It is not yet clear how the new U.S. administration will influence that dynamic. And even on the day that Obama arrived in Cuba, independent blogger and activist Lázaro Yuri Valle Roca was arrested and held in custody for five days after trying to cover a protest by the Ladies in White, an opposition group founded by the wives of jailed dissidents. The journalist said after his release that no charges were filed but that he was warned he could face legal action if arrested again.

The restoration of ties has led to suggestions from some analysts that Cuba may return to the Organization of American States, which expelled Cuba in 1962. But in June, Cuba said that as a show of solidarity with Venezuela, it would not join the group, the BBC reported. Castro's statement came after OAS Secretary-General Luis Almagro called for sanctions to be imposed on Venezuela. Membership in the OAS, whose charter includes a commission to protect human rights, would require Cuba to improve its press freedom record, including easing restrictions on internet access and ending the harassment of journalists.

■ ■ ■

Cuba, which was ranked 10th on CPJ's 2015 list of the world's most-censored countries, has the most restrictive laws on free speech and press freedom in the Americas. Its penal code contains restrictive press freedom provisions.

Most criminal prosecutions that threaten freedom of speech include charges of contempt of authority under Article 144 of the penal code, "enemy propaganda" under Article 115 or acting against "the independence or the territorial integrity of the state" under Article 91, which is often used in conjunction with Law 88, "protection of Cuba's national independence and economy," according to a 2016 comparative study of criminal defamation laws in the Americas prepared for CPJ by the law firm Debevoise & Plimpton in collaboration with the Thomson Reuters Foundation. The charges can carry a prison term of up to 20 years.

Most of the prosecutions refer to the defamation of public institutions, organizations, national heroes and martyrs, which is also often used in conjunction with other provisions to curb freedom of expression by preventing public debate and criticism of the authorities and government policies.

The far-reaching transformation of the media landscape has broadened the space for criticism, allowing all sectors of the press to delve into issues previously perceived as taboo, such as gay rights, allegations of official corruption and poverty.

The internet is perhaps the biggest hurdle for journalists seeking to become relevant, because most of their content is consumed outside the island. At the same time, they must pay high prices for online access and find original ways to disseminate their work to a home audience that is largely offline.

These new media journalists also operate in a legal limbo, in part because Article 53 bans private ownership of the press and recognizes "freedom of speech and the press in accordance with the goals of the socialist society." Many of the journalists interviewed said they approach their work cautiously and sometimes veer away from publishing overtly critical work because of the current legal framework.

Dismantling this framework for the press and removing all barriers to individual internet access while expanding it to the population at large are key to fostering a more open environment, according to analysts and Cuba experts.

The slow loosening of restrictions reflects a government that has many high-ranking leaders over the age of 80 who are not part of an active online community. Within the government and the party leadership, there is a debate on how swift this opening should be.

Dissidents, journalists who report on social issues but are not considered hostile, pro-government bloggers and members of the state-owned press all tend to agree on one point: They want the government to provide more, less-expensive and less-restricted access for Cuba's 11 million people.

In a July 2015 interview in *Juventud Rebelde*, José Ramón Machado Ventura, the second-highest-ranking member of Cuba's Communist Party, accused foreigners of trying to promote expanded internet access "not for Cuban people to communicate but to penetrate us and do ideological work for a new conquest." This stubborn approach to internet access calls into question whether the government will meet its pledge of bringing access to 50 percent of the population by 2020, finances permitting. Such an achievement will demand a great deal of courage from the Cuban leadership.

Carlos Lauría, the Committee to Protect Journalists' program director and senior program coordinator for the Americas, is a widely published journalist. A native of Buenos Aires, he has written extensively for Noticias, *the leading Spanish-language newsmagazine.*

13. Supervised Access

By Jessica Jerreat

A North Korean man walks past propaganda posters in Pyongyang, North Korea, that threaten punishment to the "U.S. imperialists and their allies."

(AP/Kim Kwang Hyon)

N orth Korean dictator Kim Jong Un's absolute grip on the flow of public information and deadly approach to dissent have made the country one of the most brutally censored in the world.

Kim, the supreme leader of the Democratic People's Republic of Korea, is the latest in a dynasty of dictators that have restricted citizens' communications and access to independent news. The media is state-owned, with the official Central Korean News Agency serving as a government mouthpiece, and the regime metes out harsh punishments for anyone accused of accessing uncensored information or sharing news from countries that it considers its enemies.

In recent years, there have been subtle changes in this dynamic that have incrementally opened the lines of outside communication. In 2012, The Associated Press was the first Western news agency to open a bureau in the capital, Pyongyang, and Agence France-Presse (AFP) announced in January 2016 that it would follow suit. Groups such as the North Korea Strategy Center, a self-described "defector-led" organization, also smuggle information into the country and try to broadcast the reality of the North Korean experience to an international audience.

The existence of a Western news bureau offers a glimmer of hope that the regime is becoming slightly less hostile to the idea of outside contact. Before 2012, the only outside bureaus belonged to North Korean allies such as China, and interviews with government officials were seldom granted. "Before the AP opened its bureau, there were virtually no images coming out of North Korea, let alone words," said John Daniszewski, the AP's vice president and editor-at-large for standards.

Since the AP established its bureau, the agency has secured unprecedented interviews with high-ranking North Korean officials, including with the foreign minister Ri Su Yong in April 2016—his first with a Western news group. Though journalists are making such inroads, they caution that the North's response is likely driven by a want for favorable coverage or to counter allegations and negative stories. Any concessions by the regime are largely inadvertent and actually belie worsening censorship.

And although the North may present a new sliver of openness to the outside world by experimenting with Western media relations, its own journalists remain strident propagandists, and advances in technology that could open up channels to independent news are fought with ever-stricter censorship measures. In addition to harsh penalties for anyone who tries to gain access to independent media, such as listening to foreign broadcasts, the North Korean government prevents access to the internet on computers and smartphones and fosters a climate of fear through the pervasive use of surveillance.

The North's media experiment is a one-way line and, as Daniszewski says, the country is "an extremely tough nut to crack." International journalists may be allowed in, but their work is not accessible to the main population, for whom the grip of censorship has only tightened.

To many Korea observers, the partial thawing of relations is less about press freedom and more a case of strategic media management as the reach of internet and smartphones threatens to undermine the internal propaganda used to subdue dissent. The government also controls media access and imposes strict guidelines. When more than 100 foreign journalists were invited to cover the ruling party congress in May 2016, Bloomberg reported that their accompanying minders were insistent about what terms could and could not be used and refused to translate overly critical questions.

Still, the feeling among journalists and Western observers is that some access is better than none.

"Sometimes it's just a matter of just being there and imbibing by osmosis, even though access is severely restricted and you are up against many challenges," Daniszewski said. "For us, not just the AP but everyone, having a few independent reporters in the country on a regular basis provides a little more window on the country."

Daniszewski, who was involved in the negotiations to set up the Pyongyang bureau when he was the AP's vice president for international news, and Eric Talmadge, the bureau chief, say that by having a steady presence there the AP has been able to cover stories that would have been beyond reach.

The bureau is staffed by a small team of international correspondents and photographers, who, under Talmadge, spend prolonged periods inside the country. The bureau also has a TV station and employs a few North Koreans, primarily as fixers. In addition to being granted interviews with Ri and other high-ranking officials involved in foreign policy, the AP's reporters have covered stories on everyday life in and around Pyongyang, including an off-beat piece on Pyongyang Zoo's dog exhibit, and serious reports on developments in the capital and interviews with the parents of a group of waitresses detained in South Korea after allegedly fleeing the North.

Among the persistent drawbacks is that international journalists on assignment are always accompanied by government minders or—as the North Koreans describe them—"guides." The host country says this setup protects foreigners in a country where strong anti-Western rhetoric is the norm.

"That's their rationale," Daniszewski said. "They say, 'Well, it's for your protection, because the people are hostile to you, and they need to understand you are there with permission.' I'm not buying it one way or the other. I'm not endorsing it, but that's what they say."

Anti-foreigner sentiments pose other obstacles to journalists beyond the government's justification for using minders. Jean H. Lee, a former AP reporter who opened its Pyongyang bureau, said, "North Koreans are educated from an early age to consider Americans the enemy, so there were certainly many times when interview requests were denied."

Talmadge, who took over the bureau in 2013, likens work-ing in Pyongyang to being embedded with the military. "Obviously the context is quite different," he said. "But in practical and psycho-logical terms, I find it very similar to my experiences embedded in Afghanistan and Iraq." As with a military embed, working in North Korea is strictly controlled. One big difference, Talmadge said, is the rationale behind how the U.S. military sets its rules for embeds. "Its attitude toward freedom of the press and its respect for and support of the work of journalists in general is obviously quite different from what I encounter in North Korea." He added, however, that, "like an embed, [reporting from Pyongyang] is one component of a broader set of reporting efforts, from other sources and places, aimed at providing the fuller picture."

For Talmadge, gaining access to sources remains one of his biggest challenges. He and Daniszewski both said the process has been getting somewhat easier and that interviews with high-ranking officials rely on formats that are surprisingly open. However, "impromptu, unsupervised access to people who are not in official positions—the general populace—is a different matter," Talmadge said. "I cannot simply go out and start talking to people as I would do in, say, Japan, where I spent most of my career as a journalist. This is frustrating and clearly limiting."

North Korea also maintains control over which interview requests are granted and requires the AP to provide an outline of interview questions in advance, though Talmadge said his reporting style has not changed. "I am free to deviate from those topics and generally do, either in follow-ups or completely different questions, as I would in any interview," Talmadge said. "Whatever the interviewee says on the record is fair game, and they understand that." He said that although he has to be accompanied by a "guide," without one he doubts that anyone would be willing to speak with him.

Talmadge said that within the obvious constraints, he is generally able to work without interference. "I have never had a complaint about a quote, nor have I ever been asked to give officials or anyone else a preview of a story before it hits the wires," he said.

The AP has been able to make inroads without compromising its journalistic ethics, Daniszewski and Talmadge said. "They don't run things on their terms," Daniszewski said. "For whatever reason, they have not tried to interfere with the content. I'm sure it's well monitored and access is severely restricted, but it has not been a case where memory cards have been taken or any notebooks demanded."

Journalists who have reported from inside North Korea's borders can only speculate about the reasons the government is granting them greater access to officials, but the consensus is that it should not be construed as a meaningful improvement in its stance toward press freedom.

Kang Cheol Hwan, president of the North Korea Strategy Center, told CPJ by email, through a staff interpreter, that although foreign journalists were being allowed to open offices inside the country, the "government continues to control the information," and any freedoms granted to AP reporters are denied to would-be independent journalists inside the country. He added that verifying information inside the country "is a challenge and can also be dangerous" and highlighted the case of a BBC reporter who was questioned and then expelled in 2016 as evidence of the regime's continuing efforts to control its image.

"Journalism in North Korea is run by the state," Kang said. "All the articles are written essentially through the party. As such, there is no such thing as independent inquiry or freedom of expression for journalists in North Korea."

Lee, the former AP reporter who is now a global fellow at the Washington, D.C.–based Wilson Center, which focuses on global issues research and dialogue, echoed Kang's view. She described North Korean journalists as being "proud to serve their country's publications" and said most had graduated from the country's most prestigious universities. "They see themselves as messengers of key party, military and government policy," she said, adding that most articles they produce focus on Kim Jong Un and other high-ranking officials. Lee said the country's press publishes little international news but that there are sections "devoted to reporting on South Korea and the U.S.—mostly anti-government protests or other controversies that fit the North Korean narrative about their enemy."

By republishing foreign media reports that perpetuate its anti-Western propaganda and ensuring that only a select few have a less blinkered view of world events, the government retains and even intensifies the control of information within the country.

Objective political coverage and international news are still off limits, Lee said. Otherwise, she noted, the average North Korean reader's tastes "are not unlike ours: Sports and entertainment are hugely popular." North Korean citizens rarely have access to an actual copy of a daily newspaper, and though television is popular, viewers often do not have adequate electricity to watch from home. Instead, most read copies of papers posted on news boards across the city or watch TV in public areas. "You'll often see people gathered outside Pyongyang's main train station to watch the news on a huge screen on the plaza," said Lee, who also teaches a class on North Korean media studies at Yonsei University in South Korea.

Kang said the party elite has access to international information through a secretive newspaper, *Chango Sinmun* (Reference Newspaper), that is circulated among the country's high-ranking officials. The paper contains a wider range of reports on foreign affairs and politics than is available to the average citizen, with stories often sourced from Voice of America, Russia's TASS agency, China's state-run Xinhua and NHK in Japan, Kang said. A segment about the newspaper broadcast by the South Korean station TV Chosun shows text on its front page stating it is for "authorized Party officials only."

Kang added that the average citizen who wants uncensored news either illegally tunes into foreign radio or relies on word of mouth. "Information passes through quite quickly in North Korea," he said. "I've found that word of mouth is quite a reliable way of spreading information. North Koreans are very interested in critical information, but in a quiet way."

Advances in communications technology are also changing how some North Koreans can gain access to news and information. Lee said the regime's elite can subscribe to the party-affiliated newspaper *Rodong Sinmun* through their cell phones or can access news via the country's intranet. As is the case with the secretive newspaper, access to the internet is highly restricted. Foreigners and Western media have access to Wi-Fi, but North Koreans who are granted permission usually have a specific task, such as monitoring coverage or researching information that can be vetted and later distributed by the state, according to Lee.

Kang described a "tension between how citizens are using technologies trickling into North Korea and how the North Korean government seeks to use and control them." In his view, "the problem is that when ordinary people access these devices and technology, they are able to have some control and access to information that they want, rather than just information from the government." A common complaint among ordinary citizens is that authorities remove the memory chips and SD cards from phones before issuing them, he said.

In keeping with Kim's efforts on the home front to appear that he is at the forefront of technology—while actually tightening control—North Korea has developed its own range of smartphones, tablets and software programs, including Red Star 3.0, an operating system that mimics iOS, Kang noted. "Ultimately, these products were carefully designed to control and monitor information," he said. Red Star 3.0 has surveillance capabilities, and the interface of the intranet, Kwangmyong, is set up to give the impression that the user has full internet access, though that is not the case. An analysis of Red Star's capabilities by the tech-focused outlet Fast Company found that its approximately 5,000 web pages mostly contain propaganda. Kang added that the country's Arirang smartphone "looks, feels and uses like a Samsung . . . but lacks the very component that makes a smartphone a smartphone. Wi-Fi, Bluetooth, YouTube, Gmail and internet browser are nonexistent."

When researchers from the German security company ERNW studied Red Star 3.0, they found it contained sophisticated surveillance properties, Reuters reported. Among the findings: If a user tries to change any part of its programming, such as disabling a firewall, the software reboots, and it also tags every document, media file or flash drive connected to a computer. "It's definitely privacy invading," Florian Grunow, one of the researchers, told Reuters. "It's done stealthily and touches files you haven't even opened."

The surveillance capability is particularly concerning in a country where the trade of flash drives containing news and other information is one of the key ways for average citizens to access news. The North Korean Strategy Center is among the groups distributing flash drives loaded with news, films and practical advice in an effort to combat North Korean censorship. Sharon Stratton, the center's program officer, told *The Guardian* the organization is careful not to include any media that criticizes the government because doing so would reinforce the "stereotype that the outside world is out to destroy North Korea."

Kang said the content typically loaded on flash drives includes PDFs of South Korean newspapers, Wikipedia pages translated into the North Korean dialect, guides on how to run businesses, radio programs and TV shows and films that show people running their own enterprises or about democracies. Movies such as *The Romantic President*, about South Korea's democratic elections, and *12 Years a Slave* and *Lincoln*, which cover the foundation of democracy in society, have also been included, he said.

Though internet access is severely restricted, the use of cell phones has been rising in North Korea thanks to a black market and porous border with China. Foreign visitors have been allowed to bring their cell phones into the country since 2013 and to use the 3G network, though the general population does not have the same level of access and is barred from making and receiving international calls, Lee said.

Anyone who seeks to buy a phone has to register with authorities, and rights groups, including Amnesty International, estimate only

3 million of the country's population of 25 million currently have access to a phone. A 2016 report by Amnesty International on North Korea's telecommunication trade said that anyone caught using a cell phone to contact a loved one who had fled risks being imprisoned. Buying a phone and SIM card on the black market is also dangerous and expensive. One North Korean who fled the country told Amnesty that SIMs could be bought for 100 yuan (US$16), which represents about a 10-month salary for an average worker.

Authorities have been quick to clamp down on such lines to the outside world through harsh new laws used to deter citizens from using cell phones. The *Daily NK*, which focuses on North Korea, reported in March 2014 that North Korea had added new clauses to Article 60 of the penal code—"attempts to overthrow the state"— which include a minimum penalty of five years of "re-education" and a maximum penalty of death for communicating with the outside world, including through cell phone contact, and 10 years of "re-education" for watching South Korean media or listening to foreign radio.

Though a sentence of "re-education" pales in comparison with a death sentence, it is still a terrifying prospect. Kang has experienced first-hand the horrors of a North Korean prison camp. When he was nine, Kang was imprisoned in one of the brutal camps after his grandfather was accused of treason. In North Korea, up to three generations of a family can be forced into hard labor for a relative's transgression. Radio Free Asia in 2016, citing testimony from three survivors of such camps (including Kang), and a former guard, reported that they are beset by inhumane conditions and physical and psychological torture are common, with detainees being beaten with branches and whipped by guards, forced to use their food bowls to collect human waste, denied rations and medical treatment and encouraged to attack one another for failing to keep up with work quotas. The government denies the camps exist.

The expansion of such restrictions and the continuing intimidation of citizens who seek independent information are evidence that, despite its efforts to appear more open with Western media, the government is simply responding to the increasing availability of communications technology.

Even with the availability of censorship work-arounds, such as sharing flash drives loaded with news, Kang said, "Once North Koreans escape and resettle, it's quite difficult for them to come to terms with the influx of information available to them." The information overload was evident when North Koreans, who, after fleeing, were provided with media training by the North Korea Strategy Center.

The idea behind the center's journalism academy was to provide nascent North Korean journalists with media training both to enhance their ability to find work and to help them inform others on conditions inside the country. Between 2011 and 2014, 286 North Koreans, most of whom had only a middle school level of education, took part in the program, and 57 of the most talented progressed to one-on-one workshops that led to the publication of their stories in the Korean-language magazine *Eyes of Pyongyang*, which covers daily life under the Kim regime. Nine interns were also placed with outlets, including *Chosun Ilbo*, *Daily NK* and North Korea Reform Radio.

"Adjusting to a more free style of reporting once they escape is very difficult," Kang said. North Korean journalists, he said, "write from a purely ideological perspective. There's no training in independent or critical thought or writing." The trainees at the academy had to "essentially re-learn from the very beginning," Kang said. "Both in style and mind-set, and what is 'newsworthy.'"

The need for such training illustrates the efficacy of the North Korean government's unrelenting censorship efforts against its own citizens. And Western journalists caution that the government's slightly softening approach toward them should not be viewed as a sea change. "I have not gotten any indication of an official shift in attitude toward more freedom of access," Talmadge said. "I do believe some parts of the government itself are experimenting with more media contact."

Daniszewski added, "When the AP started the bureau, I didn't know if it would fall apart in six months or a year. So I have a lot of satisfaction that it has gone on for more than four years. Before, it was considered audacious and unprecedented that any Western news agency could have a toehold there. After four years, I think it's become normalized." Though he acknowledged that North Korea is clearly different from countries "with a more liberal viewpoint about journalism," he said that by having a regular presence, the AP has been able to build up contacts. "North Koreans never submitted to any kind of interviews before," he said. "It's been slow, incremental work, but I think by being there, we've begun to change the environment for journalists."

Lee shared that view, saying that part of the success of the bureau is that it allows AP reporters to spend more time on the ground. "Most foreign correspondents are lucky if they make one short trip organized by the government," she said. "It's very hard for first-time visitors to distinguish between the theater and the reality—and that is how the North Koreans prefer it." Longer and more regular visits help "develop a solid understanding of what's real and what is not," she said.

The flip side, Kang said, is that although the arrival of the AP bureau has given "the world an unprecedented glimpse inside [North Korea's] borders, they have no customers inside North Korea and the government continues to impose heavy restrictions on foreign journalists."

And the danger of this slightly changing dynamic is that Western journalists also face risks when reporting from inside a country with a history of detaining foreigners. BBC reporter Rupert Wingfield-Hayes was detained and questioned for 10 hours in May 2016 after being accused of insulting the host country in his articles. In an account of his questioning, Wingfield-Hayes said he believed the government wanted to make an example of him, and before being expelled from the country, he was required to write a note of apology for his alleged transgressions.

Daniszewski said that freelancers and journalists who do not spend regular periods of time in North Korea should be cautious. Speaking generally about conditions for freelance journalists, he said North Korea "isn't the kind of place where you are likely to be a victim of random violence or mugging, but it's a highly regimented, centralized society that sees things on its own terms, and that can create risks."

The opportunity to have a physical presence inside such an oppressive country is important, however, Daniszewski said. "I know that people criticize or feel it was not worth the effort," he said, "but I believe in every case it is better to have some access than no access."

Jessica Jerreat is senior editor at the Committee to Protect Journalists. She previously edited news for the broadsheet press in the U.K., including for the foreign desk of The Times of London and at The Telegraph. She has a master's degree in war, propaganda and society from the University of Kent at Canterbury.

14. Fiscal Blackmail

By *Alan Rusbridger*

Kenyans protest extrajudicial torture and killings in Nairobi. There is a sense in Kenya today that perpetrators never face the consequences of brutality and murder.

(CPJ/Alan Rusbridger)

In some parts of the world, it is still possible to silence a journalist with a sharp blow to the side of the head. But as newspapers the world over struggle with the financial disruption of digital technologies, governments are finding new ways of controlling the press. Murder is messy. Money is tidy.

John Kituyi, a brave, persistent local newspaper editor in Kenya, was a victim of the old-fashioned method in April 2015, when the 63-year-old from Eldoret in western Kenya was killed while preparing to publish the results of an investigation that could have embarrassed leading figures in the national government.

Two assailants with a blunt object brought Kituyi's life, the story and the newspaper itself to a sudden end.

Though the threat of such physical violence remains a concern for journalists even in one of Africa's most developed nations, a less messy mechanism for constraining the free media is increasingly being used. Murder can lead to awkward questions and, if the victim is a journalist or a lawyer, may attract uncomfortable international attention. But as revenues drain away from traditional media due to the inroads of digital technologies, the use of financial-induced self-censorship, or "fiscing," can also ensure that journalists are more "reasonable" in their reporting.

Whether that was the actual motive when the Kenyan government in 2015 set up a single government agency to act as a conduit for all advertising in the country's newspapers, enabling a centralized body to turn the flow of money on or off, journalists in Kenya tell the Committee to Protect Journalists that the country's political classes are ensuring that "unhelpful" coverage will be effectively penalized, that is, that the money will dry up.

Like their counterparts around the world, Kenyan newspapers are feeling the punishing economic consequences of readers and revenues moving online. Media income from all Kenyan government sources is estimated by newspaper executives to represent at least 25 percent of advertising revenue—or it would, if the government actually paid the bills. In fact, the new advertising agency is not paying the bills. The failure of the money to arrive is, according to Tom Mshindi, editor-in-chief of the country's most influential newspaper, the *Nation*, "putting a huge amount of stress on our bottom lines, our operational, our cash flows and everything else." The second-largest newspaper group in Kenya, the *Standard*, issued a profit warning in August 2015 predicting a 25 percent fall in revenues. Other papers are also seeing sharply declining revenues.

Mshindi's former colleague at the *Nation*, Linus Gitahi, who had been CEO for nine years when he left in 2015, is no longer involved in the media business but says he is well aware of how fiscing works. Waving his wallet in the air from side to side, he says, "Oh, you're the guy who had that headline yesterday, and you want us to talk advertising this morning? Tell it to the birds."

"If they tell you two or three times, then you begin to think a little harder about the headline you put in, and, on the extreme side, you might even ask them, 'What headline will make us get back to normal?'" Gitahi says.

This is the art of fiscing: No one directly censors anyone. The newspapers respond to the potential withholding of revenue by censoring themselves.

Since independence, Kenya has at times been something of a beacon of free speech in Africa, but David Makali, a former director of the Media Institute in Nairobi and a prominent commentator on the press, compares the present situation with the era of former President Mwai Kibaki ("a bit oppressive, but subtle") and that of Daniel Arap Moi ("brutal suppression").

Today, Makali says, "These new guys have basically taken to co-opting journalists. They've perfected the art of censorship because they intervene at the very inside using the state levers of advertising and manipulation through resources to make sure that you won't publish anything they don't like. You publish; the sanctions are immediate."

According to Makali, "If you are not in the good books with the government, they throttle you. They've done that successfully. So they combine direct intimidation, economic strangulation and infiltration. They respond with a hammer, withdrawing support to newspapers, and this intimidation has completely devastated journalism, the standards that we are used to—and we had quite some good standards of investigative reporting." Today, rather than a watchdog that barks in warning, "We have a media that is basically squeaking," he says.

One attraction of fiscing is that it is difficult to prove that a newspaper self-censored as a result of financial pressure. That star journalist who didn't have their contract renewed? A government spokesman will shrug his shoulders and say it has nothing to do with him. Most, though not all, editors are too proud to admit that they will quietly suppress a particular story for fear of losing revenues.

But high-profile editorial figures have been dispatched from their jobs in recent months following work that did not please Kenya's highest level of government, known as State House. As a result, important stories remain untold or neglected.

Kituyi is not the only member of the media to have lost his life; yet, senior journalists, many of whom were granted anonymity during interviews, confess that they now soft pedal investigations they think the government will disapprove of for less physically menacing reasons. In short, they concede that fiscing is working.

The health of the Kenyan media matters particularly on a continent where truly free speech is rare and becoming rarer still. The journalism coming out of Nairobi since independence in 1963 has often been robust and relatively unfettered. Compare the country's newspapers even today with those in the neighboring countries in the region, and the Kenyan press still shines, if not as brightly. There is a fairly new constitution and, until now, a Supreme Court willing to take account of it.

But ask Denis Galava, a former senior editor at the *Nation*, about how he lost his job after writing a New Year editorial that displeased State House. Talk to Gado, one of the world's most trenchant cartoonists, who learned that his contract at the *Nation* was not renewed this year after he upset politicians in Kenya and beyond. Sit down with Robert Wanjala Kituyi and hear him recall in a whispered voice the investigation that led to his own harassment and his brother's murder. Ask editors and reporters why almost no one in the Kenyan media has aggressively sought answers over military reverses against the jihadist terror group Al-Shabaab. A picture emerges of a press that is feeling economically uncertain and editorially intimidated, a situation that has worsened since CPJ found in a 2015 special report that Kenyan leaders were not upholding their commitment to freedom of the press.

In this constricting media environment, fiscing is the new form of intimidation. According to Eric Oduor, secretary general of the Kenya Union of Journalists, the Jubilee government, which took its name from the 50th anniversary of independence and has been led by Uhuru Kenyatta since 2013, "is quite smart in how it is doing its affairs but, more or less, they're just doing what [former President] Moi used to do, only that, given that it's a new era and maybe this is a modern society, they are not doing it in a crude way, the way Moi would do. . . . They deny media houses revenue from advertising. They are, basically, trying to tell the media that you either do what we want, or we shut you down. Exactly, that is what is happening."

A leading editor who asked not to be named says, "This government is very hypersensitive here about criticism. They're in a very dominant position, and they're trying to roll back a lot of the constitutional reforms and centralize government and strengthen the executive presidency, so it has made for difficult times. I would think that all the newspapers have pulled in their horns, to some extent."

The government's extreme sensitivity to criticism has its roots in the 2010 decision of the International Criminal Court, or ICC, to prosecute the current president, Kenyatta, and his deputy, William Ruto, over the violence that erupted following the 2007 elections. The troubles broke out after Orange Democratic Movement leader Raila Odinga was denied victory under controversial circumstances. He was on course to win the election, but, at the eleventh hour, and to general disbelief, Mwai Kibaki was announced the victor.

The official death toll in the violence was put at 1,200 people, with 500,000 people displaced. In the subsequent ICC investigation, then-Deputy Prime Minister Kenyatta faced five counts of crimes against humanity, including inciting murder and rape. Ruto was charged with being an "indirect co-perpetrator" with members of the Kalenjin ethnic group in murder, deportation, torture and persecution in and around his hometown of Eldoret.

U.S. President Barack Obama lent his support to the charges, urging Kenya's leaders to cooperate fully with the ICC investigation. Once in power, post-2013, Kenyatta and Ruto had other ideas. They not only rejected all the allegations but denounced the ICC as "the toy of imperial powers." The case eventually collapsed after many witnesses withdrew or, in some cases, disappeared or died. According to the ICC, no fewer than 17 witnesses against Ruto alone withdrew their testimony.

How did the Kenyan media cover this situation? Initially, the *Nation* supported the ICC, declaring in a 2010 editorial: "No one has ever come as close as [ICC prosecutor Luis Moreno-Ocampo] to slaying the dragon of impunity in Kenya."

But once Kenyatta and Ruto came to power in 2013, the story became more difficult to cover.

"The view, which we put in our editorials, was these are legal proceedings, let them go to their logical conclusion," says then-editor of the *Nation*, Joseph Odindo. "If you're cleared, we're happy, we'll celebrate with you as our president. If you're found guilty, then deal with the consequences but don't try to sabotage the legal process; it shows a disrespect for the law. Now, the fact that the media did not stand with them and did not support their efforts all became a source of a grudge, for both of them."

John-Allan Namu, an investigative reporter who set up an online-based independent investigative operation after leaving Kenya Television Network, says of the stories of witness disappearances, interference and murder: "If told definitively . . . it would be one of the most explosive stories yet, considering how many people died in the post-election violence. But who is this person who is going to go up against the president and the deputy president in trying to prove, or trying to just get to the true facts of what happened?"

■ ■ ■

One editor who was interested in getting to the facts was John Kituyi, who started his own newspaper, the *Weekly Mirror*, in Eldoret after becoming frustrated over stories that never saw the light of day at his previous employers. His persistence in investigating corporate power had landed him in jail for months for criminal libel in 2005 after he wrote about alleged human rights violations at a factory. Kituyi employed his brother, Robert, who was nearly 30 years his junior, to investigate the case against Ruto, even though the elder Kituyi and Ruto had once been close friends.

To try to get to the bottom of the story, I meet Robert Kituyi for lunch at an Italian restaurant in a shopping mall near the center of Nairobi. He wears jeans and a black T-shirt bearing the words "I'm an ACTIVIST and proud of it." It is a feature of Nairobi's geography that the restaurant—which is otherwise typical of those found in any European capital—is 10 minutes away from the Kibera slum, where 200,000 people live mostly without electricity, fresh water or sewerage.

Robert eats little as he embarks on a long narrative about how he and his brother—whom he insists on calling "my editor"—patiently cataloged the proceedings of the ICC case against the most powerful politician in the region. Softly spoken anyway, he drops his voice to barely more than a whisper as he tells the story of how the two men orchestrated the ICC coverage.

Robert's investigations led him to visit the ICC headquarters in The Hague to inquire more closely of the prosecution team about aspects of the case they were building against Kenyatta, Ruto and others. Each story they ran was met with complaints, and John would regularly tell Robert "people are not happy about it . . . the Kalenjin tribe are not happy with what we are saying."

"It was not an environment that allowed one to operate freely," Robert Kituyi says. "The community was getting hostile, but we kept going. My editor would tell us: 'I survived the harshest years of Moi, you guys are lucky. We have space for freedom of expression.' So he kept pushing us, he kept reassuring us that, so long as your articles were factual, he'd stand by us. That's what kept us going—that reassurance."

There came a point in the ICC investigation when the prosecutors said they would consider using evidence from witnesses who had dropped out of the case. Robert was intrigued about what this meant for the likelihood of convicting Ruto. He says he was in close contact with a former *Nation* journalist, Walter Barasa, for whom the High Court of Kenya, in cooperation with the ICC, issued an arrest warrant in August 2013, which claimed that he had tried to corrupt three ICC witnesses. In May 2014, Kenya's Court of Appeal blocked the arrest warrant on the basis that it was an abuse of judicial discretion, saying the High Court had barred Barasa from presenting certain pieces of evidence as well as an oral argument on his behalf.

As Robert pursued the story, he says he began receiving serious threats on his life. Two strangers approached him in a restaurant in late December 2013 and told him to back off the story, adding that they knew where his kids went to school and how to find his wife. A few days later he was again warned off the story by two other strangers. Both groups claimed to be from the Directorate of Criminal Investigation but did not produce IDs, he contends.

A few days later, when Robert was out shopping with his wife in Eldoret, he realized he was being followed. He says he tried to report the situation to the local police but they refused to take his statement. By now he was seriously frightened and left town for a week.

Robert lowers his voice even further as he tells of another attempt to report his fears. When a policeman texted him to set up a meeting, he wondered: Was it a trap? They eventually met. The policeman, who was from another district, advised him "as a brother" to leave town immediately. Robert said he did not need persuading and relocated his family to Nairobi. "Many citizens in Eldoret fear Ruto a lot," he whispers. "Even the police officers fear the deputy president. They really fear him because he's one of those basically powerful people in the region."

Robert continued to cover the story from a distance. In late 2014, Meshack Yebei, an ICC witness whom Robert had interviewed, disappeared and a mutilated body was found shortly afterward in a river in Nandi County, some 500 kilometers northwest of Nairobi. His ears had been chopped off, his eyes gouged out, his tongue cut off and his genitals severed. The *Star* reported that he had been abducted by people who pretended to be ICC investigators in SMS messages to his mother and a friend.

Robert's reaction, he says, was, "Wow, that was so close."

The body was identified by relatives. But in a further twist to the story, the identity of the body was contested and, according to John Kituyi, who spoke with mortuary attendants, had been switched with another body. A body that was purportedly Yebei later turned up near Mombasa. John Kituyi resolved to set out this narrative of alleged witness interference in two pieces in consecutive editions of the *Weekly Mirror* at the end of April 2015.

The first story hit the streets on April 25. The next day, John Kituyi told his younger brother that it had upset people, and he then set about preparing his second story. The two men spoke again on April 29. It was their last conversation.

At 8 p.m. the following evening, Robert received a call from one of his sisters telling him that his brother was dead. By the time Robert got to his older brother's laptop in the newspaper office in Eldoret, the hard drive was missing. His brother's head and two front teeth had been smashed by something heavy and lethal, and the final story had disappeared. Soon afterward, the newspaper closed. More than a year later, there has been little progress in the case. A man allegedly in possession of John Kituyi's SIM card has pleaded not guilty to robbery.

The case against Ruto was finally dropped in April 2016. The Gambia-born ICC prosecutor in charge of the case, Fatou Bensouda, admitted that the ICC was ill prepared for protecting witnesses in such situations.

"It became very complicated in the end," Bensouda said in a June 2016 interview. "Not only were the witnesses pulled away from the case, but there were even attempts at interfering with their family members. . . . If you are going to protect witnesses against the whole community they come from, that is quite a challenge."

For Robert Kituyi, who dares not return to Eldoret, the fear lives on. "If they're going to kill, they will come," he says quietly. "I'm a believer of God, we will meet the true judge—God himself. That's all."

I ask Robert if he has been widely interviewed by his fellow Kenyan journalists. He shakes his head. "I will tell you this, I have talked to many journalists after this killing, and they will tell you they do not want to do stories like this. They say there's no story worth my life."

■ ■ ■

Godfrey Mwampembwa, who goes by the name Gado, is the best-known cartoonist in East Africa. Tanzanian by birth, he abandoned studies as an architect after entering a cartoon competition run by the *Nation* in Nairobi. He joined the paper in 1992 and has been ridiculing politicians for the *Nation* and its sister paper, the *East African*, ever since. "He's a very brilliant cartoonist, probably second only to Zapiro in South Africa," says one envious rival editor.

Gado's trademark is to find a visual gag (often very offensive) to identify his subjects. Uhuru Kenyatta, son of the founding president, Jomo, was a young, inexperienced politician when he first took office, so Gado drew him in diapers and with a feeding bottle.

When the ICC pressed charges against Kenyatta and Ruto, Gado began caricaturing the president and deputy president with a penal ball and chain attached to their ankles. After Ruto was caught up in a property scandal and claimed that the land in question was owned by Sikh businessmen, Gado began depicting him in a Sikh turban.

Other Gado cartoons caused offense. Ruto failed to see the joke when Gado pictured him aboard a private jet, "the hustler's jet," being pampered by four beautiful women. Ruto, again depicted with his ball and chain while being massaged, had been on a whirlwind tour of African capitals trying to whip up opposition to the ICC.

Then, in January 2015, Gado drew a cartoon of Tanzanian President Jakaya Kikwete in a similar pose, surrounded by beautiful women, three of whom were labeled Cronyism, Incompetence and Corruption.

Gado, a stylish, striking man with a white-flecked beard, wears a multicolored, checked scarf draped over his shoulders when we meet for coffee in a central Nairobi hotel, and he smiles broadly as he discusses such troublemaking cartoons.

"Cartoons are always seen as a barometer of a free press," he says. "A drawing can say things that are not easy to say using other mediums. You know, you can always get cartoonists to tell you 'Up you' in a way that probably an editorial editor would not."

That, he thinks, has particular importance in Africa. "Just being able to put that mirror and say, 'This is how you look.' In Africa, we are coming from a culture whereby the leaders are used to being clapped. Leaders are not used to being criticized and laughed at. . . . It's one of those mediums that really says, 'Look, you can actually speak your mind and you can actually criticize leaders, and it is fair to do so.' And by doing that, you are actually really standing up for lots of other people."

But Gado has found that this freedom in Kenya is not what it once was. He has always been accustomed to pressure from the political classes but says that editors in the past defended him, even if they sometimes asked him to drop a particular visual gag.

"The paper was always behind me, even when I've been sued for libel," he says. "We've always had, like, negotiations. An editor might say, 'Look, Gado, why don't you just go easy on these guys', you know, 'just give it a while.'" We developed a relation that was very workable with my editors. At the time, they never ordered me to do anything. If a cartoon was more sensitive and they've dropped it, I've used it online. I didn't mind that. I understood the background and where we had come from."

Gado's former editor, Joseph Odindo, confirms this pattern of behavior, and says he eventually persuaded Gado to drop the baby diapers for Kenyatta. "We got complaints about that. So I persuaded him to come up with another image, because, actually, to be fair, it was not relevant anymore. He had grown in politics, he was no longer an acolyte of Moi and he had managed to be president."

Odindo, who is an experienced old hand at journalism now editing at the rival *Standard*, confirms there were further complaints about the depiction of the ball and chain. "Now that became an issue, it was, 'We were making fun of a very serious situation,' and again they didn't like it. The message was clear: 'Look, this is not a laughing matter.' I had a long battle with Gado over that [and] he eventually abandoned it."

After the hustler jet cartoon, Odindo says, "The deputy president was mad, he was angry. They sent messages. They actually called about it. He was not happy, but it was factual; it was true, right. And the cartoon just rubbed the salt on the wound, but he never forgot."

Also, Gado says, "I started getting feedback from editors: 'Look, they don't really like this chains and balls you do, they are not very happy about it.' And I had reached a point whereby Odindo actually had to sit me down and say, 'Look, I think I've reached the end of the road here, Gado, I think the board has intervened.'"

Gado says he also received phone calls from Ruto's press secretary protesting the use of the Sikh turban. When he continued to draw it, the calls went to his editorial bosses, including the CEO. He also believes the group chairman was called.

"Did Ruto complain? Yes, he did," confirmed the former CEO, Linus Gitahi. "Did Uhuru complain? Yes. Did they complain about

other things? Absolutely, for nine years, and Gado did a lot of bad
things in the nine years, really, a lot of bad things. And actually, if
there is a guy who kept me awake at night from politicians, it's Gado,
because he kind of just used to get them at the sweet spot, bad."

But what did it for Gado in the end was the Jakaya Kikwete cartoon. The Tanzanian government's response to the satire on its president was swift and sharp: It banned the *East African* from distribution
in the country, claiming to have suddenly discovered that the paper was
unregistered.

The *Nation*'s initial response was to defend the cartoon, with the
chairman, Wilfred Kiboro, denouncing the ban as "unfair and undemocratic." But behind the scenes, the reaction was less robust.

Linus Gitahi faced a dilemma. The paper had 40 employees in
Tanzania. Did he ditch them or "deal with Gado"? His solution was
to offer Gado a year off on paid leave. "I told Gado, 'this guy is literally
asking for your head, right? What we do is we give him your head, in
the sense that we give you a study leave. If there was ever a time you
wanted to write a book, this is it.'"

Gado was not displeased to be allowed a full-paid yearlong break.
Within a week of the cartoon appearing, the *East African* published
a groveling apology for depicting the Tanzanian president in "a bad
light." The drawing "should not have been published except for a rare
lapse in our otherwise rigorous gatekeeping process," the editorial
noted.

Honor was satisfied. But it was eight months before the *East African*
was allowed back on the streets of Dar es Salaam. And Gado had an
unpleasant shock in store.

■ ■ ■

During Gado's absence from cartooning, relations between the government and the press hardened. The next flare-up came at the 2016 New
Year, while Gado was on his forced sabbatical. This time, the problem
was an editorial in the Saturday edition of the *Nation*.

The offending piece, an editorial known as a "leader" and framed
as a personal letter to Kenyatta, was written by Denis Galava, a soft-
spoken, erudite 41-year-old who had worked in a variety of senior

executive positions, including editorial writer, since joining the *Nation* in 2010. In the absence of senior editors, many of whom were on holiday, Galava says, he discussed the theme with colleagues before writing it on Friday.

The piece, which Galava said took him about 30 minutes to write, began bluntly: "Your Excellency, 2015 was a bad year for Kenya. All the pillars of our nationhood were tested and most were found wanting. Some collapsed, some were seriously weakened, while others were desecrated beyond repair."

Galava says other colleagues read the editorial before it was printed. He thought little about it before going home. He'd written more critical editorials and four New Year leaders before. This one didn't seem a particularly big thing.

His mood changed the following morning after the editorial started to trend on social media. "My senior colleagues began calling me and saying that the board chairman is livid," Galava says. His colleagues told him that people from State House had been demanding to know who had written the editorial. "They were asking, 'You tell us who was working yesterday, who's this trying to sabotage us?'"

According to Galava, his colleagues told him that State House was threatening to speak to the Aga Khan, an important Shia religious leader and the main shareholder in the *Nation*. By Monday, Galava had received a call from a friend in State House: "Denis," Galava recalls the person saying, "I'm really sorry to tell you this, that editorial, you are going to be suspended at least—but you are toast, it's really unfortunate."

It was unusual, to say the least, for a journalist to be informed of his impending defenestration by a government official, and before the newspaper had even convened an inquiry into what had happened. But the prediction turned out to be accurate: Galava was, indeed, toast.

Galava soon heard that his editors were describing the editorial as "a rogue act." Within days, the CEO of the *Nation* was on the BBC comparing Galava with a bank teller who steals money when his seniors were not around. Galava was sacked. He is now suing the company for wrongful dismissal.

The Nation's current editor-in-chief, Tom Mshindi, says he is reluctant to be drawn into the case because of the forthcoming legal action, but he denies receiving any calls complaining about the article and says, "Just suffice it to say that there were some procedural things that were not followed in terms of the way we do clearances on matters that are published and, particularly, very sacrosanct things like editorials."

One former *Nation* editor, who asked not to be named, says there is no way the paper would have sacked Galava unless someone complained. "When the shit hits the fan, you've got to stand together," the person said.

Another rival editor, who likewise asked not to be named, believes that if Galava had simply criticized the government he would have survived. His mistake was to have addressed his criticism at the president.

Charles Onyango-Obbo, a former managing editor of the *Nation*, says he was astonished that his old paper chose to name Galava as the writer of the anonymous editorial leader. "For you to then somehow detach yourself from that responsibility, I mean, that was disastrous. I have never seen anything like that," he says.

■ ■ ■

The Nation is still a very profitable newspaper, earning US$22 million in profits after taxes in 2015, down from $27 million the previous year. But, as with all newspapers, circulation is falling. Galava reckons the *Daily Nation* (the weekday edition) is now selling around 130,000 copies compared with 170,000 to 180,000 in 2013. Gitahi believes the newspaper has three to five years before digital disruption begins to seriously bite into its revenues.

As traditional revenues decline, the leverage of government increases. "There's no way *Nation*, or any media house in this country, can survive without government advertising," says David Makali.

Many observers of the Kenyan media scene believe further pressure is being brought to bear on the *Nation* via the Aga Khan, who bought the paper in 1959 and still owns 38 percent of the stock.

For decades the Aga Khan, who has diplomatic status, was treated like a head of state whenever he visited Nairobi. In addition to the *Nation*, he has numerous other business interests in Kenya and is the spiritual leader of the Ismaili community—the world's second-largest Shia community, which regards the Aga Khan as the 49th direct descendant of the prophet and, in Kenya, includes a prominent thousands-strong business network.

When the new Jubilee government came to power in 2013, many people began to notice a difference in how the Aga Khan was treated. It was rumored that he was kept waiting for a long time before being granted an appointment to see the new president, that the government canceled a number of privileges that he had previously enjoyed, and that Ismaili businesses had begun to feel unwanted pressures and attention from government.

One veteran editor says the new government decided to play hardball. "It's hard to bend the *Nation* to a point where it would subordinate its journalism totally to the government's interest," he says. "The government can put pressure on the *Nation* through these other interests of the Aga Khan, and I think that's what may have happened."

The same editor praises the Aga Khan's record on standing up to pressure, but says: "What's at stake here are the interests of so many people who look up to him as a spiritual leader. And then what is causing all these problems? Media. The *Nation* used to be a huge contributor in the early years to the community's coffers, but no longer."

A rival editor reads the situation the same way: "I think the Aga Khan bows to pressure. And, you know, the thing about these guys here is they're so tough and ruthless, and you saw the way they more or less destroyed the ICC. Kenya has really damaged the ICC, massively, and you know they just really play hardball . . . and they also played hardball with the Aga Khan." Essentially, he says, the government put pressure on the ICC and the Aga Khan, who then put pressure on journalists.

Charles Onyango-Obbo agrees with that assessment. "My own sense is that the biggest source of pressure for journalists is around stories that cause problems with the Aga Khan's business interests," he says.

A representative of the Aga Khan, speaking on condition of anonymity, agreed, saying, "Yes, there have been lots of unpleasant efforts through the years to influence the direction of *Nation* coverage—especially when the political climate has been as polarized as it has been in Kenya of late." But, he added, "When the Aga Khan learns about any such pressures, from any source, he insists that they be taken directly to the independent board and management of the company.

I do not recall a time when the Aga Khan has interfered with the *Nation*'s independent editorial judgment."

Galava has little doubt that the pressure on the *Nation*—both through advertising and on the Aga Khan's wider interests—is being felt. "If you speak to people in the Aga Khan community, in the Ismaili community, they often will tell you why the *Nation* has become a liability." He says that when he was managing editor, the staff was told by a senior executive, "I'm not telling you this to censor you, but I'm just giving you the picture."

"But the thing which is, which now everyone knows in Kenya whether inside or outside the *Nation* or the *Standard* or the *Star*, that you can't touch the president. The consequences of touching the presidency are dire," Galava says.

■ ■ ■

This hardening of the government mood was disturbing for Gado as he approached the end of his sabbatical. By then, both the former editor and the former CEO, Joseph Odindo and Linus Gitahi, had moved on. In February 2016, just a month after Galava's suspension, Gado was told he wasn't wanted back at the *Nation*. He says colleagues told him he had been "marked." His 23-year career with the *Nation* was over.

Mshindi, who broke the bad news to Gado, chooses his words carefully when asked about the decision to terminate Gado's contract. "This is not a decision usually taken by one person; this was a collective decision that was taken by more than just one office, because he was a very senior person, I mean, at a certain level, people do get involved. I can't just wake up, myself Tom, and start sacking editors. It's not done that way."

Does that mean that the decision was made by the editorial board? "Well, it's a management decision," Mshindi says. "The board is a policy making organ; it doesn't come into these decisions."

Asked whether such a decision would normally fall under the purview of others, such as the CEO or chairman, he says, "Exactly, those kinds of people. I mean, especially the CEO and myself and, you know, HR."

After his sacking, Gado—who is now back working for his old boss, Odindo, at the *Standard*—drew a cartoon titled "The Media without Clothes," which shows several identifiable naked Kenyan media executives scrambling for money in front of the regally clothed figures representing the president and vice president.

Asked to explain the drawing, he says, "They're being compromised. They have abdicated their role. What you have is the president dishing out money and some people of the media sort of collecting the money . . . I challenge you that you can take that drawing and ask any journalist worth his salt about the state of play of the media in Kenya and probably you would have 90 percent among them who said, 'Yeah, that's what's happening.'"

The firings of Gado and Galava, combined with fiscing, have affected staff morale at the *Nation*, and one very senior executive says, on condition of anonymity, that the newspaper has had to plead with the government's advertising authority to be paid the money they're owed. "Inevitably, it has an impact on stories," he says. "The guys on the second floor [the commercial department, which includes advertising] come along and say, 'These stories you are writing are making it hard for us.'"

Once newspaper management appeared to give into government pressure, the belief spread that stories critical of the corporate world would be similarly unwelcome. All the editors and senior executives I've spoken with, for example, say they would not think of running a negative story about Kenya's largest corporation, Safaricom, for fear of losing advertising revenues.

The senior *Nation* editor says: "We're retrenching, so there's no security of jobs any more. Everyone understands there are no jobs out there. If the government paid us what they owed us, then that would help. But the message goes out loud and clear . . . go easy on government and corporates. Reporters get the message. They understand what stories are off limits so they go for safer stories."

Officials with the Government Advertising Agency (GAA) readily admit that the agency owes media houses a great deal of money. Dennis Chebitwey, director of public communications at the Ministry of Information, Communication and Technology, who runs the GAA, estimates the agency owes media houses more than 5 million pounds, adding, "But that will be paid." The *Nation*'s Tom Mshindi estimates the debts could actually be up to twice that sum. Chebitwey insists he has never called an editor either to complain about coverage or to influence the way they report.

■ ■ ■

On January 15, 2016, Al-Shabaab militants attacked and overran a Kenyan army base in the town of El-Adde in Somalia—one of Kenya's largest military defeats since independence in 1963. Yet the only public acknowledgment of casualties has been the publication of photos of the return of four flag-draped caskets. There have been no published accounts in Kenya of how many Kenyans were really killed in the raid or whether, as some international journalists have reported, Kenyan commanders ignored warnings and were ill prepared for the attack.

In a self-congratulatory video posted to YouTube, Al-Shabaab claimed that more than 100 Kenyans were killed. Other accounts, including from the Somalia government, placed the death toll at between 180 and 200.

The lack of coverage is baffling to many reporters. "It's a huge story . . . it was a time of huge crisis for the military, forget the human cost for a moment, big as it is," says John-Allan Namu, the former TV news journalist who set up an online-based independent investigative operation. "Think about what it means for the esteem with which we hold our military, even going down to the reasons why we went in."

Mshindi, at the *Nation*, says he wishes the government would be more forthcoming but defends his own paper's reticence, adding, spikily: "You guys sit in Washington and Paris, and you can report these things with a certain degree of, I don't want to use the word 'casualness,' but 'distance.' You can throw around any numbers that you want to throw around. I cannot do that."

Namu believes some of his colleagues have held back for fear of being seen as unpatriotic. But he also thinks some journalists fear that they'd be targeted if they do—"perhaps not physically targeted but, you know, be the source of isolation, attacks by people who are supportive of the government, so called 'patriots,' and that can be tough for a journalist to be able to walk it alone, even though your facts speak for themselves." He recalls his editors being extremely uncomfortable about the coverage of terrorism. "From early on we found out that it's because they were constantly under pressure from government to have these stories not told and have a more patriotic theme around the coverage of terror attacks. Our CEO told us the kind of calls that he was getting, from who, which offices, and basically what he was being told."

Odindo says that "in private discussion with generals, they would tell us that, look, El-Adde was just mismanaged, totally mismanaged, the commander slept on the job. But they couldn't be quoted officially, and you are not on the front line, so you can't say that. The closest we came to it was quoting the Somali president, who had to eventually apologize to the Kenya government and withdraw. Now that's a foreign head of state. What would they have done to a media house, which had no proof?"

■ ■ ■

My first opportunity to ask for an official figure comes when I meet with State House spokesperson Manoah Esipisu, a former Reuters reporter who studied journalism at City University in London. Dressed in a gray sweater, he tilts back in his chair in an office on the first floor of the whitewashed former official colonial residence of the governor of East Africa. The room is dominated by five television screens on which he can monitor multiple Kenyan TV channels at once. Today, only one is on, showing a Nigerian "Nollywood" soap opera.

Esipisu begins by extolling the strengths of the Kenyan media, together with the government's firm belief in freedom of expression. "We are certainly the most open society in our region, and we are certainly one of the most open, if not the most open, on the continent," he says. "We have a long history of a strong, if sometimes activist, media, and it is something that both the media and ourselves would like to protect."

Asked how he defines the term *activist*, he says, "Sometimes the media takes on causes fairly quickly, some justly, some, in our view, unjustly," then adds, "The views that we think are unjust, that's what we think is activist."

Nearly every journalist I have met since arriving in Nairobi considers the current president and deputy president extremely thin-skinned. Esipisu flatly contradicts this: "Here, at the presidency, certainly, we don't really mind criticism, however harsh, provided it is reasoned out.

So, if you tell me I'm a piece of shit, you need to say how you've come to that conclusion so that when I read the stuff, I understand truly they wouldn't have gotten to any other conclusion but the one they got to."

I ask him about the charge that the GAA is being used to put pressure on media houses. He acknowledges that perception is out there but insists it would be "foolhardy" for any government to behave in that way. The reality, he says, is more mundane: The government has a huge budget deficit, and the GAA is not the only official department struggling to pay its bills.

We move onto the sacking of Gado. Esipisu denies the government caused it and distances himself, in words that seem to have been carefully chosen, from the idea that this had anything to do with pressure from government. "I haven't seen any evidence of such pressure, even though I have heard stories of that pressure," he says. "I think that it is easy to say 'State House did this' . . . but, ultimately, it comes to proof. I mean, this building doesn't make phone calls, people do. The administration did not ask for his sacking."

"Did the administration complain about him?"

"Actually, no. . . . Of course, this does not preclude the fact that people, privately, might have called people that had their friends within the newsrooms and said, 'Oh what's this type of stuff we are seeing?' or 'What direction are you guys going?' I think you can't preclude the fact that people will call others they know in newsrooms in just the same way I would call him and say, 'Look, geez, this thing I saw on Saturday, you guys are crazy,' something like that. But is that exacting any pressure? I wouldn't say so."

What about the sacking of Denis Galava?

Esipisu becomes more assertive, claiming that Galava replaced an editorial that was already typeset and ready to print—something that no one in the *Nation*'s management has said.

"Galava did what people, ordinarily, don't do in a newsroom, replacing an editorial that is already plated without consultation—that's what I hear," Esipisu says. "But would I ask that he be fired for that? No, I wouldn't. That's an internal management thing. If you publish stuff that you can't stand by, that's a problem."

He says he has never known of a case in which a newspaper has been involved in a public discussion about who wrote a particular editorial. "And so, if I was furious, I'm furious with the newspaper. I'm not furious with the leader writer. I wouldn't know who the leader writer was . . . so, I would say those are internal governance lapses, for which somebody has had to take responsibility, rather than pressure from the outside."

Were there, in fact, calls from State House over the editorial? "I wouldn't say whether, I don't know whether—I can't speak for everyone," Esipisu says. "I can truly say, since I speak for the president, I'm sure he did not make any such calls in relation to that article." He added, "If you ask my personal reaction, was I angry? Yes, I was. You can attack people, but you still must be respectful. If you have argued a case properly, no one is going to worry about what the issues are; you have argued the case. A leader is not a forum for abuse, especially for a head of state. So, yeah, as the president's spokesperson, I had a view. That view was not expressed."

When the interview moves on to Kenyan casualties at El-Adde, Esipisu loses his fluency for the first time and shifts uncomfortably in his chair. Asked how many Kenyans died, he says, "I don't have a number, it's the Department of Defence." Can he provide a rough idea? "I have no rough idea," he says. "I know that they have said. No, they haven't said how many people died, they have told us there might have been two companies, and I don't know how many died. I don't know how many survived, so I can't say that on the record."

I suggest that some have put the number of fatalities at from 180 to 200.

"The Kenyan government has never given a figure for the deaths in El-Adde," he says.

How could the government possibly have no idea of the number killed? "The Ministry of Defence must have its reasons, and I defer to them," he says. "I don't know the figures." Asked what reasons the ministry might have, he moves around in his chair again. "I haven't taken a view on that," he says. "The ministry has said it's got good reasons, so, if the Kenya Defence Forces say this is what would be good for us, we go with what they are saying, in terms of what they think would be useful for the team's morale and the fact that they remain in those spaces."

■ ■ ■

The legal framework in Kenya has always represented an uncomfortable challenge for journalists, with many complaining about the use of libel laws, including criminal ones, to suppress their work. But the Jubilee government has, since 2013, tried to introduce further laws and regulatory mechanisms that could, if fully implemented, further erode the ability of the media to aggressively report.

On January 16, 2016, Joseph Nkaissery, the Interior cabinet secretary, which is essentially the national security minister, ordered the arrest of anyone circulating photographs or video of the El-Adde attack. Several bloggers were briefly detained following this edict.

The Security Law Amendment Act (SLAA), part of which was ruled unconstitutional, would—if passed in full—severely restrict journalists' ability to report on terrorism. Another proposed law, still being litigated in the courts, amending the Kenyan Information and Communications Act (KICA) would create a new media regulator with some members appointed by the government itself. Journalists may now face fines of up to 500,000 Kenyan shillings and media companies up to 20 million shillings if the new regulator finds them in breach of a government-directed code of conduct.

Both measures have been opposed by international free speech organizations and have been the subject of challenges in the courts. Parts of the SLAA were ruled unconstitutional by the High Court in February 2015; the same court ruled that aspects of the KICA and Media Council Act were constitutional on the grounds that they placed limitations on reporting national security issues. Both judgments are currently being appealed.

Most of the editorial figures I speak with in Kenya say they are extremely anxious about the run-up to the next election in August 2017. "Now that we're going into the elections, I think that political pressure is going to be open, very direct," Odindo says.

Namu agrees. "I see that legislation as being open for abuse, especially at very sensitive times in our country's progression," he says. "In spite of its problems, the media still remains one of the more trusted institutions in the country. But institutions like the Supreme Court seem to have started to fall down a bit in terms of the credibility test. The electoral body has unanimously been declared by both sides of the political divide to be one that doesn't stand the test of credibility.

So you head into an election with all of this being unresolved after the five years of political tumult that we've had here. And you wonder whether the media won't be targeted."

While in Nairobi, I attend a street protest against the extrajudicial torture and killings of Willie Kimani, a young human rights lawyer, along with one of his clients and a taxi driver, sometime around June 23, 2016. Kimani's skull and genitals were reportedly crushed. Numerous Kenyan lawyers, dressed in suits adorned with purple ribbons, turn out for the demonstration and subsequently go on strike for a week.

Perhaps because the entire legal system rebelled against these brutal killings, the murder was investigated and four police officers were charged. But the talk at the demonstration is of impunity—the sense that, in Kenya today, no one ever faces the consequences of such brutality and murder. The nongovernmental watchdog Independent Medico-Legal Unit reports that the Kenyan police killed 97 people in 2015 alone.

Charles Onyango-Obbo believes the collapse of the ICC case against the country's two most powerful politicians showed that no one is really held accountable. "The postelection violence has ended without any [significant] convictions . . . and I'm just wondering what lesson that has sent," he says. "I think the lessons most people seem to have taken away from that is that you can get away with it. And so, you know, going forward, I'd just like to say I don't think the future looks promising."

Linus Gitahi agrees. "Anything that's happened to lawyers can happen to journalists—like that," he says, snapping his fingers.

A May 2016 High Court ruling on a new raft of government legislation affecting the media observed that Kenyan journalists were "not to put too fine a point on it, not angels." More than one editorial commentator cautioned that the Kenyan press must take responsibility for some failings of its own. A Western observer of the Kenyan media who asks not to be named cautions against having too rosy a view of the incorruptibility of Kenyan journalists and claims to have seen evidence of "brown envelopes" delivered to journalists who are on the take. David Makali tells me the political parties have spies and journalists on the payroll in all newsrooms. An editor in Nairobi agrees that this is likely.

State House's Manoah Esipisu digs into his own experience at Reuters and observes that, in his opinion, newsrooms are losing institutional memory. Investigative reporting and business reporting are in decline, and the reasons cannot all be laid at the government's feet, he argues.

Wycliffe Muga, a columnist with a long personal memory of journalism, thinks government attempts to suppress the media are cyclical and that "in the end, the media always wins because as a collectivity we are much stronger than them."

But that strength in the past relied on strong financial footing, which enabled newspaper managements to shrug off any attempts to influence editorial decisions by financial manipulation. Today, fiscing is one of many tools that can be used against the free media in Kenya, and in some cases, the mere potential for its use results in censorship.

The editors and reporters with whom I speak are divided over whether a degree of accommodation with the government is just a fact of life for journalists in contemporary Africa. One editor describes the compromise he struck after State House "went ballistic" over a story that was critical of the president. "They demanded a retraction," says the editor, who, like many, fears being quoted by name, which is indicative of the state of the free media in Kenya and the potential for government repercussions. "They demanded an apology; they demanded who'd done it. We were told if we didn't give them the source we would lose all government advertising. In the end, we said, 'Look, we're not going to do that, but we'll give you a pledge that we will never again do that kind of personal, what might be interpreted as a personal criticism of the president, we won't do those things.' It was a deal."

Joseph Odindo, who has seen a lot in his long career, agrees that there are unwritten laws. "Traditionally, the Kenyan media has always known that there was an invisible line which you don't cross—or you cross at your peril," he says. "And that's with all previous governments we had. So part of the challenge of being an editor is knowing whether to cross, and, therefore, how you get around it; you publish without crossing that line."

Linus Gitahi, who is generally admired by his former colleagues for the way he protected them, has a similar view. "Actually, in Africa you've got to do that, you've got to manage," he says. "It's a question of how you navigate the landscape."

Namu recalls being told by a senior editor, "This is a great story, great story, but do not challenge the president." He says, "It was made clear to us, I'll never forget those words."

But can such accommodations survive the age of social media, where millions of ordinary Kenyans now have access to unmediated and largely still unregulated content? Charles Onyango-Obbo believes the old rules cannot survive much longer. "In the past, most of the editors would be people who have connections to the president, or ministers and, you know, a lot of these things could be ironed over quietly at a dinner, at the club. There has been a social change so that is no longer possible. I think it has become very, very, difficult to sustain with everyone seeing what they are seeing on social media or digital."

Bloggers, including on a site called Owaahh, are getting noticed for investigations that are taking mainstream media by surprise. John-Allan Namu, who is 33, is part of the younger generation of Kenyans who have decided to move into new media to be able to work freely. "To be fair, our executives did try to defend us, but I think the pressure became too much," he says. "I sort of made up my mind that, if I am going to be able to develop as a journalist, I can't do it within the context of a mainstream media house." Namu's new venture, called Africa Uncensored, has eight employees and is supported by donors and supplemented by content sold to media houses.

"Part of our Kenyan culture, a resilience and a resistance to wrongdoing and to encroachment on rights—that hasn't yet disappeared," Namu says. "And, I mean, this country has so much potential. Geographically, alone, we are equidistant from so many places in the world. We have great weather. We've got a great service industry. But it's our rulership and, you know, some of the vices in society that are holding us back. There are a lot of people who either want us to speak about it or are doing something about it themselves, so I'm hopeful."

But in the end, Namu wonders how his little start-up will fare when "the rubber will meet the road and we have something that's just untouchable." He talks about the recent murder of Jacob Juma, a gadfly businessman and frequent user of social media who in January predicted his own death on Facebook for "my stand over corruption in gov't." He was shot 10 times as he drove home to a Nairobi suburb on May 5, 2016.

In the past, the financial strength of the mainstream media would have conferred a level of protection upon reporters, Muga believes. But now, many journalists working for large media groups feel less confident of protection, and those on the outside feel very vulnerable.

The Kenya media—still, for all its frailties, a point of relative light in a troubled region—is discovering what it's like when a government exploits the financial fragility of the press today. In that sense, Kenya may prove to be a different kind of beacon.

Alan Rusbridger was the editor of the Guardian *from 1995 to 2015. He was editor-in-chief of Guardian News & Media, a member of the GNM and GMG boards, and a member of the Scott Trust. In October 2015, he became principal of Lady Margaret Hall, a college in the University of Oxford.*

15. Right Is Might

By David Kaye

Political cartoonist Zunar, shown accepting CPJ's International Press Freedom Award in 2015, faces the possibility of dozens of years in prison as a result of his cartoons attacking Malaysian Prime Minister Najib Razak.

(CPJ)

Yevgeny Zamyatin's strikingly original 1920s Russian novel *We* gets read far less than its canonical English-language descendants, *Brave New World* and *1984*. Yet George Orwell knew of and clearly drew from Zamyatin's book in creating *1984*. The homage-paying is obvious: A solitary hero struggles to define himself in relation to society; a state and its mysteriously cultish leader control privacy, information and thought; love is prohibited and freedom is categorically rejected; the violence and brutality of power lurk beneath a seemingly clean and mechanized society; common words are redefined and propaganda is pervasive in daily life; and, in total, reality is rejected in favor of myths and lies.

On the first page of *We*, which is set hundreds of years into a dystopic future, the hero, known as D-503, records in his notebook a proclamation found in the *One State Gazette* about the building of a great spaceship. The proclamation announces that the ship soon "will soar into cosmic space" in order to "subjugate the unknown beings on other planets, who may still be living in the primitive conditions of freedom, to the beneficent yoke of reason." The proclamation goes on, "If they fail to understand that we bring them mathematically infallible happiness, it will be our duty to compel them to be happy."

"But before resorting to arms," the proclamation magnanimously adds, "we shall try the power of words."

D-503 gradually recognizes that reality varies from the word of the governing One State, whose plans for extraplanetary subjugation reflect what it has already accomplished on Earth. He comes to resist the theology behind the One State rejection of freedom, and the novel extrapolates from what was, for Zamyatin, the contemporary abuses of early Bolshevism to draw a direct connection between information control and the elimination of privacy and the fundamentals of political liberty.

Though the book was written almost a century ago and is set centuries into the future, its core conflict seems particularly timely: 2016 gave us repeated opportunities to reflect on the core ideas of freedom rejected by any number of states. That is not to say that any one government's behavior in 2016 mirrored the single-minded totalitarianism of the One State, but the novel's themes could not be more relevant to our current situation, in which governments and non-state actors repeatedly throttle, suspend or entirely cut off the flow of information, redefine language to the detriment of reportorial fact-finding and attack those responsible for keeping us educated and able to engage in discourse about matters of great public interest.

As this edition of *Attacks on the Press* demonstrates, governments worldwide are threatening the flow of information, whether through online restrictions, physical attacks and harassment, the abuse of legal processes or the enactment of overly broad rules of law. Those actions rest on the same premises of power and insecurity that dominated the One State: If the people are given the tools to figure out the truth (or *a* truth) for themselves, governmental power will weaken. The more corrupt and greedy the pursuit of power, the greater the incentive for people in authority to limit public debate and access to information.

Few doubt that such authoritarian tendencies are on the rise, resulting in direct attacks on the practice of journalism. But unlike in Zamyatin's world, we have a network of international legal protections guaranteeing the rights to seek, receive, and impart information and ideas of all kinds, regardless of frontiers and through any media, including Article 19 of the International Covenant on Civil and Political Rights. States have the authority to restrict such rights only when the changes are rooted in law and when they are considered necessary and proportionate to achieve a legitimate objective. However, within this framework of law and the institutions designed to protect it, dozens of categories give cause for alarm or even panic (which is how my October 2016 report to the U.N. General Assembly was received).

The following are the five most notable categories that are having a direct impact on journalism and journalists.

Traditional censorship

Traditional censorship is alive and well around the world. Some governments promote theories of why their citizens cannot access information, such as public order or morals, resulting in such infamous tools as the Great Firewall in China, designed to limit online information for Chinese citizens. Other governments are disrupting internet and telecommunications services, often without any explanation, usually during public protests or elections, shutting down entire networks, blocking or throttling the speeds of websites and platforms and suspending telecommunications and mobile service. Access Now documented more than 50 shutdowns in 2016, though I suspect the number is even higher.

Outside of digital space, other governments require that specific myths be told and retold in the media and educational textbooks. Some states' laws enforce official narratives by criminalizing breaches of public solidarity or "misinformation" or "false news." While the problem is undoubtedly exacerbated by the failures of internet search engines and social media to deal with those gaming their systems, I am afraid that the age-old problems of propaganda and what many in the United States call "fake news" could result in just the kind of restrictions that oppress individuals in authoritarian regimes.

There are also softer forms of censorship in democratic societies involving pressure to adhere to government narratives. Donald Trump's attacks on journalists are notable in this regard and are serious causes for alarm. In Japan, I found that a variety of factors—government pressure, media concentration, a tradition of access journalism and a lack of journalistic solidarity—combine to establish norms of censorship and self-censorship.

Terrorism

One of the gravest threats to expression today is rooted in the reality of terrorism and threats to national security. Nobody should doubt that states have an obligation to protect life against groups such as the Islamic State and other terrorist organizations. Yet states often use the grounds of antiterrorism, counterextremism and national security as broad bases to limit the flow of information. Turkey has become a leading practitioner of such an approach to attacks on the media. Of course, genuine incitement, demonstrated terrorist recruitment and suppression of legitimate secrets can all be handled through mechanisms of law, including criminal law. But we see much more than that. The reliance on counterterrorism serves as a catchall to throttle or shut down the media and justify the detention of journalists, bloggers and others. My colleagues in the European, inter-American and African systems and I addressed this issue in our annual joint declaration of 2016 because it is one of the predominant themes of restriction globally. In the text of that declaration, we expressed alarm over what we described as:

> the proliferation in national legal systems of broad and unclear offences that criminalise expression by reference to [countering and preventing violent extremism], including offences "against social cohesion," "justification of extremism," "agitation of social enmity," "propaganda of religious superiority," "accusations of extremism against public officials," "provision of information services to extremists," "hooliganism," "material support for terrorism," "glorification of terrorism" and "apology for terrorism."

We also emphasized the importance of adherence to human rights law:

> States should not restrict reporting on acts, threats or promotion of terrorism and other violent activities unless the reporting itself is intended to incite imminent violence, it is likely to incite such violence and there is a direct and immediate connection between the reporting and the likelihood or occurrence of such violence. States should also, in this context, respect the right of journalists not to reveal the identity of their confidential sources of information and to operate as independent observers rather than witnesses. Criticism of political, ideological or religious associations, or of ethnic or religious traditions and practices, should not be restricted unless it involves advocacy of hatred that constitutes incitement to hostility, violence and/or discrimination.

Legal restrictions

States are adopting legal proscriptions designed to do away with criticism. Some states punish "propaganda against the state" or "insult" to the states' leadership. Others penalize sedition, targeting those who criticize the state or its leaders, such as the Malaysian cartoonist Zunar, who faces the possibility of dozens of years in prison, and who is currently subject to a travel ban as a result of his cartoons attacking Prime Minister Najib Razak. Often, critics are punished on grounds of disrupting public order or on the basis of so-called lèse-majesté laws or criminal or civil defamation lawsuits.

Governments are increasingly pressuring internet platforms to take down critical content, among other things. Twitter, like other major internet platforms, publishes a regular transparency report that underscores the extent to which states are seeking takedowns. Some material may be taken down legitimately on grounds of incitement to violence or genuinely actionable defamation. Such takedowns should always require the intercession of judicial authorities, but often they do not.

Surveillance

In *We,* the "numbers" (i.e., citizens) live in glass apartments and are given one hour a day to draw the curtains for personal time. Today, we see a marked increase in surveillance that is not based on reasonable suspicions of criminal activity nor authorized by the rule of law. We see at least two other forms of surveillance that undermine the confidence we can have in our communications, our browsing history online, our associations, our sources and research and so forth.

In 2013, Edward Snowden famously disclosed the abuses of mass surveillance conducted by the United States and the United Kingdom. In the past year, France, the United Kingdom and even Germany—an erstwhile champion of policies strictly limiting the state's snooping powers—have considered or adopted new, intrusive measures of surveillance. In the case of Germany, legislation failed to provide protections for journalists. The U.S. government has been advancing problematic forms of social media monitoring at the border, with serious potential consequences for foreign journalists.

But they are not alone. Russia's Yarovaya Law, China's Cybersecurity Law and Pakistan's Prevention of Electronic Crimes Act, all adopted this year, impose surveillance of communications trafficking their platforms.

In the context of such measures, states are also cracking down on the tools that can provide individuals with a modicum of privacy, such as encryption and anonymity designed to protect journalists, activists, minorities, dissenters and others. Increasingly, states seek to limit the availability of such tools precisely because they interfere with surveillance.

Meanwhile, states that might not have such technical advantages have been able to purchase software on the open market to conduct targeted surveillance of activists, journalists and ordinary citizens. For one example, I filed an amicus brief supporting the position of the Electronic Frontier Foundation, which is currently suing the government of Ethiopia on behalf of an Ethiopian-American activist whose computer in the U.S. state of Maryland was infected with malware and surveilled for nearly six months by Addis Ababa.

Digital distortion

From a normative perspective, we remain at an early stage of thinking about human rights in the digital age, but even so, private actors own and control what many of us think of as public spaces. They have hundreds of millions of individual users—or in Google's and Facebook's cases, billions. They are proud of that, as they should be. They run businesses and make a lot of money and create a lot of jobs.

They also manage expression—they take down content, mediate what's permissible, decide the information that we might see. It's all quite opaque, hidden by proprietary algorithms and uncertain human input. Meanwhile, they have terms of service that are usually not drafted in order to advance human rights norms. Perhaps that is acceptable, because of course they are private enterprises. But when information and access require membership in these social media giants, to what extent can they hide behind the wall of private enterprise? To what extent does the private sector owe a responsibility to ensure access not merely to information but to fair, nondistorting information? Is law an approach that does more good than harm? There is reason for concern and monitoring, because what we increasingly see are walled gardens, where individuals get only the information the platform permits.

As noted, we are seeing various echoes from the politically minded dystopic novels of the past in the rejection of the depicting or arguing about reality. And it will get worse unless we name the problem, organize to resist it and ultimately use the tools provided by human rights laws at national, regional and international levels to address it.

In *We,* Zamyatin chuckles at "one of the absurd prejudices of the ancients—their notion of 'rights.'" Here is what he says, and it's both a clear-eyed view of the rhetoric of the powerful and the necessity of resisting it:

> Suppose a drop of acid is applied to the idea of "rights." Even among the ancients, the most mature among them knew that the source of right is might, that right is a function of power. And so, we have the scales: on one side, a gram, on the other a ton; on one side "I," on the other "We," the One State. Is it not clear, then, that to assume that the "I" can have some "rights" in relation to the State is exactly like assuming that a gram can balance the scale against the ton? Hence, the division: rights to the ton, duties to the gram. And the natural path from nonentity to greatness is to forget that you are a gram and feel yourself instead a millionth of a ton.

The year 2016 should provide us with a renewed opportunity to remind ourselves that we yet have the tools to assert ourselves not as grams to be weighed against the tonnage of the state. We need to protect and reform the institutions we have, to ensure that they work to protect rights, that we move to a place where we can celebrate and criticize the world as it is, or we think it is, not as our leaders want us to perceive it to be. That's what the practice of journalism is all about.

David Kaye is the U.N. special rapporteur on the promotion and protection of the right to freedom of opinion and expression. He is clinical professor of law at the University of California, Irvine, School of Law, where he teaches international human rights and humanitarian law and directs a clinic in international justice.

16. Eluding the Censors

By Karen Coates

Young men check their Facebook pages at a restaurant in Yangon, Myanmar, over beers and dinner. The social network is improving access to news in remote areas.

(Jerry Redfern)

S queezed between China and Vietnam, Phongsali is the north-ernmost province of Laos, a land of mountains, valleys and iso-lated villages that is home to more than 15 ethnic groups. As recently as a few years ago, news traveled through Phongsali at a pace akin to regional traffic: slowly, on a bumpy route rife with potholes and disruptions.

The communist government of Laos keeps tight reins on all print and broadcast media, and newspapers rarely make it this far north. Many people, in fact, do not read, and until recently, there were few phones or TVs.

Then came Facebook. No longer was news limited to established routes, which in the years since has provided locals with a convenient work-around when it comes to censorship by the communist govern-ment. Though that work-around carries its own perils, including some-times questionable vetting of facts and the threat of retribution from the government, it has changed the censorship dynamic for good.

With an influx of smartphones, the face and pace of life in rural Laos has likewise changed, as has the way Laotians learn about the world around them. In 2010, I spent a week in a Phongsali village and had virtually no connection to the outside world. Power was limited to small batteries and generators and the roads were dirt. In March 2016, I returned. The highway was paved and electricity towers lined the main road. The land felt different. And it was.

I sat one night with colleagues at a dusty roadside restaurant after a long day of reporting in the field. We drank Beer Lao while awaiting orders of minced-meat salad and sticky rice. The table was mostly silent as our Lao companions were deeply engrossed in their Facebook feeds, heads bent down, faces creased with consternation. There had been another shooting (in a spate of recent attacks) against a public bus trav-eling a major north-south highway. My companions watched video of the aftermath and then chatted online with family and friends. When our food arrived, we discussed an undercurrent of violence that had shaken the country.

This conversation would not have taken place without this remark-able shift in rural information—through Facebook.

Social media, and especially Facebook, is changing journalism like nothing before, particularly in places where public information has historically been stifled or hard to find. "During the turbulent times, Facebook becomes the easiest and quickest place for its users to disseminate news, see and instantly upload photos, videos, and then share them with whoever you want in a format that is accessible everywhere," observed Aliya Bashir, an independent journalist in Kashmir. The result is that citizen journalists have a new voice that never existed before. "The media in Kashmir isn't what it used to be," Bashir said. "It is being reborn, and with this rebirth, we are witnessing the death of government-controlled media as we knew it. The emergence of Facebook has rocked the local and Indian national media field to its foundations."

In September 2016, U.S. President Barack Obama mentioned the change in a speech to the Lao people in Vientiane. "We want to be your partner with the young people of Laos as you strengthen your communities and start businesses, and use Facebook to raise awareness for the rights and dignity of all people," Obama told the crowd.

Emily Bell, director of the Tow Center for Digital Journalism at Columbia University, summarized a significant concern about that proliferation in a recent talk to a University of Cambridge audience. The rapid predominance of social media, she said, is happening "almost without us noticing, and certainly without the level of public examination and debate it deserves."

Facebook launched in 2004 with a mission to "give people the power to share and make the world more open and connected." Twelve years later, it's a media giant, alternately portrayed as either the "savior" of journalism or its "destroyer." When Facebook first emerged, it represented a "radically democratizing" shift in journalism that "helped amplify new voices whose opinions and experiences had never been part of mainstream media before," wrote tech journalist Annalee Newitz.

"In many cases, Facebook information guides mainstream media because it tends to be really fast and far-reaching," said a former freelance journalist and Vietnamese press consultant who asked to be identified only as "G.V." because, she said, she's precluded from stating public opinions in her current job with an embassy staff. Vietnam has one of the world's worst press freedom records, but social media is helping citizens circumvent government restrictions. G.V. cited a recent case involving allegedly corrupt hospital guards in cahoots with transportation companies. Facebook video footage showed Hanoi hospital guards preventing a vehicle from taking a dying baby to the child's hometown hospital. "News outlets brought this forward to the relevant hospital's leaders, who completely denied the case," G.V. said. But after another video was posted "from another angle, which clearly shows that the guards were at fault," she said, hospital authorities were forced to take action by firing the guards.

Based on scale alone, the world's biggest social media network presents unparalleled opportunities for reporting. "Facebook is a Rolodex of 1.7 billion people" who could be potential sources, witnesses, experts or leads on a journalist's research and reporting, said Vadim Lavrusik, founder of the platform's journalism program. And it's not just a boon to journalists. Citizens "now have the power to be a mini-news bureau," Lavrusik, who led the Facebook Live engineering team, observed. They can reach audiences that were previously available only to what he calls "gatekeepers such as media organizations or government-sponsored agencies."

Today's journalists also use Facebook to vet and connect with sources. When *InSight Crime* senior researcher Deborah Bonello plans reporting trips in Mexico, she wrote in an email, "I generally reach out to people via FB to make an initial contact with them. That way they can see my profile, website and connections and know I'm legit." And she can research the same about them.

Activists use Facebook in similar ways. "It helps me report about my organization and my own activities; it helps me to communicate with people," said Long Kimheang of the Housing Rights Task Force, a Cambodian group that works with Cambodia's urban poor. Calling, chatting, sending and uploading photos and video, storing and retrieving data are all possible through Facebook. When she started her work in 2010, Kimheang said, she couldn't communicate so fluidly with the public. "It was very hard before, when Facebook was not very common," she said, adding that radio and TV "are owned and controlled by the government and rich," and there was no outlet for grassroots organizations like hers. Now, she has more than 2,500 Facebook friends around the world, many of whom are professional contacts and supporters.

But Facebook is also a for-profit company (a huge one, at that) and operates accordingly. "Facebook will do what is best for Facebook," wrote *WIRED* staffer Julia Greenberg. More and more, the company is nudging media producers to turn away from their traditional pipelines and publish directly on the platform. No longer is Facebook just a distributor of news; it's a major gatekeeper in its own right, with all the powers to publish, to censor and to shape society's views.

The ubiquity of Facebook, and other forms of social media, leads to critical questions about accuracy. As Bashir noted, fact-checking is a challenge. Anyone can post anything to Facebook without any qualifications, training "or, for that matter, any proof," she said, which contributes to the spread of misinformation, exaggeration and propaganda.

The "fake news" phenomenon hit home in the U.S. during the 2016 presidential campaign, when Facebook and other forms of social media were used as launchpads for rumors and lies about Hillary Clinton, Donald Trump and their supporters, all of which blazed across the internet. The spread of such falsehoods can have dire consequences: In December 2016, a North Carolina man who opened fire in a Washington, D.C., pizzeria later told police he was on a mission to investigate what was, in fact, a false election-related conspiracy theory.

There are also questions about how Facebook determines what's trending and what's in readers' best interests to see. When leaked documents revealed in May that Facebook employs human editors, analysts reacted with deep concern. Those humans, it turns out, operate "like a traditional newsroom, reflecting the biases of its workers and the institutional imperatives of the corporation," Michael Nunez wrote for *Gizmodo*.

One critical difference between traditional publishers and Facebook is that editorial decisions seem to be made in a "black box, inaccessible to the public," Chava Gourarie wrote in the *Columbia Journalism Review*.

"The problem is not that there are human decisions affecting the shape of the public sphere—this has always been the case," wrote Robyn Caplan of the Data & Society Research Institute. "The concern is that these decisions are in the hands of a small group of often invisible actors who can shift these priorities at will."

Many accuse Facebook and its subsidiary, Instagram, of censoring content under the murky guise of "community standards." Those standards nominally prohibit images of bare breasts, profane language, hate speech, pornography and criminal activity. But critics also note the removal of posts pertaining to plus-sized women, breastfeeding mothers, breast cancer awareness campaigners, teen sexual health organizations, indigenous rights activists, conservative journalists, pro-cannabis groups, museum exhibitions and drag queens.

While some bemoan the broad powers of Facebook to censor content, journalists—and citizens in general—face individual physical dangers when using social media. Many governments have arrested citizens for content they post online. In May, Thai authorities arrested the mother of a student activist for allegedly insulting the monarchy on Facebook with a one-word reply to a private message. The word? *Ja*, an affirmative that essentially means *yes*.

In Israel, authorities have arrested dozens of Palestinians—and some Israeli Jews—in the past year for "incitement" of violence based on Facebook posts. In India, two girls were arrested for Facebook postings after the death of an extremist leader. When Priyanka Borpujari, an Indian journalist, wrote an op-ed for *The Boston Globe*, half a world away, friends warned her to be careful, although the piece was unsigned. "It was very easy to know that I had written it," she said. "I am definitely much more careful about what I post out there on Facebook."

In Laos, authorities arrested three citizens who posted allegedly anti-government Facebook posts. Months later, Radio Free Asia reports, the government is on the hunt for Facebook friends of the three, who, at the time of this writing, had not been charged. Under a 2014 decree, internet users face harsh jail sentences for criticizing the ruling party online.

This was not the first incident involving Lao censorship of Facebook activities. A few years ago, the survivor of a plane crash that killed several prominent Lao politicians posted details of the event shortly after it happened. "That posting disappeared in 10 minutes," according to a longtime expatriate in Vientiane who wished to remain anonymous.

Beyond government censorship and threat of arrest, Facebook users are open to trolling and harassment—which can range from mean to abusive, with lasting repercussions.

None of this is entirely new. Journalists on the ground have faced harassment, intimidation, arrest, rape, torture and threats with guns and knives for as long as the profession has existed. And in many cases, real-life dangers outweigh the online versions in both the fear factor and the real-life consequences. "I was incarcerated briefly, I was beaten up by the cops, had my camera taken," Borpujari said. "It had definitely left a big impact on my mind." The dangers she faces online "are nothing compared to being on the ground and being a person who's living there."

Borpujari explained what it's like to work in conflict zones in India, such as Kashmir, a northern region involved in a longtime territorial dispute between Pakistan and India, which has led to a fight for independence, and Assam, an eastern state where insurgents have fought a decades-long separatist movement. "The moment you land in there, the whole state knows . . . because you are not part of them," Borpujari said. She claims police have monitored her phone calls and placed her under surveillance. "Information travels so fast in a conflict area," she said, and it's "not because of social media. It's simply because that's the scenario in a conflict situation."

Repressive regimes have always had ways of tracking people, just as they've also had ways of manipulating information. That hasn't changed—but Facebook offers yet another method.

Myanmar (formerly Burma) presents an interesting case study. For decades, under the former military junta, many citizens had little access to information beyond government control. Every newspaper required a license to operate and every story underwent scrutiny by state censors. There was, essentially, no daily news in the old Burma; every publication was weekly. And almost no one had a mobile phone.

Then, within a couple of years, SIM card prices dropped from US$2,000 to less than US$2. The transformation was immediate and widely apparent: Cell phones appeared nationwide in teashops, train stations and remote village homes. The citizens of this vast and diversified country were suddenly linked by technology as never before.

But there is a downside. "Social media platforms like Facebook have become fertile new ground for hate speech," Nick Baker writes in the *Myanmar Times*. Hate speech—through songs, pamphlets and other forms of propaganda—is a long-standing facet of communication across the conflict-ridden country. "While this material was once con-strained by resources, manpower and geography, the advent of explo-sive internet connectivity has meant an unprecedented new reach," Baker wrote.

In 2012, Myanmar was engulfed in anti-Muslim furor—directed mostly at minority Muslim Rohingyas—which resulted in 250 deaths and the displacement of about 140,000 people. Since then, analysts say, Facebook has served as a vehicle for spreading hate speech, though it also sparked a counter "flower speech" campaign. In one exam-ple, in 2014, radical nationalist Buddhist monk Ashin Wirathu, who is well known for his anti-Muslim rhetoric, posted on his Facebook page the fabricated allegations that two Muslim men had raped a Buddhist woman in Mandalay. The post went viral, and Mandalay erupted in violence as Buddhist mobs tore through the city's streets, pillaging businesses. Two died and dozens were injured. Unrest among Rohingyas and violent reprisals by the army continued in parts of the country in late 2016.

Meanwhile, "media literacy" and the ability to distinguish between truth and fiction have not kept pace. "Hate speech is 360 degrees," said Ye Naing Moe, head of Burma's Yangon Journalism School. "Anti-military, anti-Bamar, anti-ethnic, anti-Muslims, anti-Buddhists." Distinguishing fact from fiction is critical, he said, and "ordinary people in the neighborhood really need to know how reliable the informa-tion they receive from social media and even mainstream media are, and how they can check them."

When Facebook Live was launched in 2015, it allowed those with access to stream in real time. With a good connection, audi-ences can simultaneously watch anything from a Florida piano player to an Afghani barbecue to the latest in video news from Lower Egypt. The new tool "enables us to see news as it's unfold-ing by giving people the power of a TV camera on their mobile phones," Lavrusik said.

It's a notable shift, and it's happening around the world.

It was Facebook Live that allowed millions to view the death of Philando Castile, who was shot by Minnesota police in July 2016. His girlfriend, Diamond Reynolds, posted live video of the immediate aftermath, as an officer kept a gun pointed at the couple while Castile was dying. American audiences were already accustomed to viewing cop shootings online—but until then, longer after the fact.

Livestreaming presents new opportunities for censorship, too. In August, Facebook complied with Baltimore County, Maryland, police requests to deactivate the social media accounts of 23-year-old Korryn Gaines, who posted video of an altercation with officers before they shot and killed her, as she was barricaded in her home with her 5-year-old son. One of her videos remains on Instagram while others are reportedly archived as evidence, no longer viewable by the public. Baltimore officials justify the move as a means of preserving "the integrity of the negotiation process with her and for the safety of our personnel [and] her child."

■ ■ ■

A dozen years on, Facebook is a primary outlet for news in many countries, and the questions for journalists are not so much about the "ifs" or the pros and cons of social media. Social media is now a given. The questions now hinge on how society is responding to dramatic changes in communication and how journalists incorporate those changes into their reporting.

"I think it's easy to define someone like me as a 'social media journalist,' and I've always thought that was missing the point," said Andy Carvin, the founder of reported.ly, a groundbreaking platform designed to cover news almost entirely through social media. Carvin, who was dubbed "the man who tweets revolutions" for his social media-based coverage of the Arab Spring, sees vast opportunities in combining the strengths of new and traditional reporting tools and platforms. "For my entire career, going back around 22 years now, I've been interacting with people online and offline to help me better understand complex ideas and explain them to the public," he said. That's the bedrock of any good journalism. "Fundamentally, it's not about the platforms," he added. "It's about the willingness to develop relationships with communities."

Borpujari agrees. She thinks social media can—and should—be used for more nuanced reporting about human stories. It's ironic, she said, that people often embrace a more democratic or holistic form of online storytelling when it comes to our pets, as opposed to our fellow human beings. "We watch dog videos where the dog is being funny, when the dog is being naughty, when the dog is being sleepy, when the dog is being hungry. But we don't show humans in that vast plethora of emotions or vast plethora of experiences, right?" she said. When it comes to stories of people, social media gives us "quickies," she said. "Whatever is exciting."

But the dog videos prove social media can offer more. She gives the example of an Instagram series she started after her father died "as a cathartic way for me to deal with loss." It sparked a following that spurred a conversation about the loss of parents "and how we don't talk about that." When Borpujari posts long missives and personal essays, people respond with "their most generous and most surprising comments," she said, "reacting in very beautifully surprising emotions."

That was apparent to me on that night in 2016 in northern Laos, at the little roadside restaurant in Phongsali, with dinner beginning in silence and all those downward-facing heads and thumbs scrolling through Facebook feeds. It seemed an anachronistic scene in a remote little pocket of a sparsely populated country, where showers are cold and meals are cooked over wood fires. But when the owner served us fiery plates of food and another bottle of Beer Lao was cracked, we all started talking—about the future of Laos and worries over this recent spate of violence, which no one was able to adequately explain.

We shared a meaty, reflective conversation—in three languages— spurred entirely by the news on Facebook. And in that case, everything reported was true, and it was widely known despite the government's routine efforts to censor the news.

Karen Coates is an independent journalist and senior fellow at Brandeis University's Schuster Institute for Investigative Journalism.

17. Zone of Silence

By Robert Mahoney

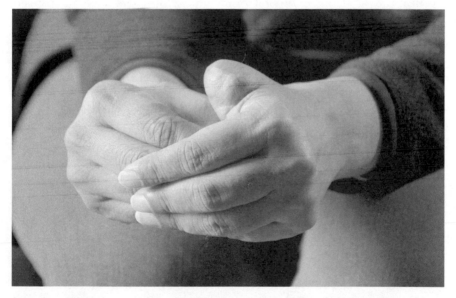

Rafida Ahmed lost her thumb during an attack by extremists that killed her husband, blogger Avijit Roy, in Bangladesh's capital, Dhaka.

(Reuters)

J ournalist Avijit Roy founded the blog Mukto-Mona, or Free Thinker, as a forum for free expression and ideas that challenged the growing religious intolerance in his native Bangladesh. His blog for intellectual freedom cost him his life.

The U.S.-Bangladeshi blogger and his wife were hacked and stabbed by suspected Islamist extremist assailants as they left a book fair in the capital, Dhaka, in 2015. Roy died; his wife was critically injured.

The brutality of the attack and the prominence of the victim shocked the country, but there was more to come. Four other bloggers were hacked or stabbed to death that same year in separate incidents, again by suspected extremists. No one has been prosecuted.

The barbarity of this unprecedented wave of attacks has achieved its aim: the silencing of unwelcome voices. Bloggers who have been threatened have left the country or dialed back their criticism, according to Bangladeshi journalists.

This tactic of murderous intimidation has been used with similar chilling effect by other groups of religious extremists but also by purely criminal gangs.

The self-styled Islamic State (IS) in Syria and Iraq has specialized in gruesome executions of journalists, from beheading foreign hostages and posting videos of the murders on the web to lashing local reporters against trees as a warning to residents.

In Mexico, drug cartels hung the bodies of social media users from a bridge and staged a macabre tableau with the beheaded body of a social media activist as a warning to others who would report on or criticize their operations.

The killings are the ugly embodiment of censorship in states where the rule of law has either been eroded or collapsed and is being replaced by codes enforced by criminals or religious and political fanatics.

The political, cultural and religious differences among South Asia, Mexico and the Levant are obvious, but for a number of journalists and bloggers in these regions, censorship through extreme violence is a daily reality. The consequences for the audiences served by those reporters are the same: a zone of silence. The public is robbed of independent information, and in the case of IS, is fed "news" tailored to advance the interests of the group alone.

Censorship has always stalked free expression. From ancient China through imperial Rome to the Alien and Sedition Acts of the would-be tyranny-free United States, governments have behaved as if it is their duty to uphold public order and morality by curbing expression and criticism. Thus, when Saudi blogger Raif Badawi "defamed" religion in 2012, it was the Saudi state that ordered him imprisoned and flogged.

But in Bangladesh, machete-wielding thugs took it upon themselves to silence what they considered the religious slander of Avijit Roy. Fanatics of various stripes have also long threatened journalists, but their numbers are growing, and states are failing to rein them in. Impunity in the murder of journalists is one of the biggest challenges facing the media, especially in the Global South, according to CPJ research. In the past 10 years, only 3 percent of the murders of journalists have resulted in full justice with the masterminds convicted. In the same period, political groups, including IS and other extremist organizations, are the suspected perpetrators in more than 40 percent of murder cases. One of the reasons for the upsurge is simply that killers know they will get away with the crime. With little likelihood of a criminal penalty, religious extremists or drug lords have only a political calculation to make. And for many that calculus is easy—murder a few prominent journalists with headline-grabbing brutality, and the rest of the press corps will be intimidated into self-censorship or silence.

This has resulted in so-called violent non-state actors—militias and organized crime, insurgent and terrorist groups—becoming as much a threat to press freedom and the lives and liberty of journalists as repressive regimes.

Governments, at least in theory, are accountable to the people they serve and the international commitments they sign. They can be influenced by international mechanisms such as the United Nations, the Inter-American Commission on Human Rights system and advocacy organizations holding them to those obligations. Neither the Islamic State nor the Zetas cartel play by those rules, and they certainly do not receive delegations from independent journalists' unions or freedom of expression organizations.

Islamic State and Al-Qaeda and its many affiliates have a new twist on the propaganda of the deed with their high-profile attacks and bombings, including the kidnapping or murder of journalists from the deserts of Syria to the office of a satirical magazine in Paris. They use social media and other new communication platforms to promote the attacks as tools for recruitment or intimidation.

Western journalists are learning what reporters in much of the rest of the world have known for years: that they are at risk not only on the battlefield but also in their own homes and offices.

Between them, Algeria's insurgent Armed Islamic Group and Colombia's various rebel, paramilitary and criminal groups killed scores of journalists in the 1990s in an attempt to control information. But that was pre-web and social media. For most Western audiences, the narrative arc of violent censorship and intimidation begins with the 2001 Al Qaeda–linked kidnapping and beheading of *Wall Street Journal* reporter Daniel Pearl in Karachi. It continues through the 2006 death threats against Danish daily *Jyllands-Posten* in retaliation for publishing cartoons depicting the Prophet Muhammad to the 2014 beheadings of U.S. journalists James Foley and Steven Sotloff by IS in Syria and the massacre of eight *Charlie Hebdo* journalists in France in 2015. The IS beheadings sent a shockwave through the news industry and effectively made IS-held territory off-limits to Western news organization staffers and freelancers alike. This has made much of the world reliant on local Syrian activists and citizens-turned-journalists for news from inside the self-proclaimed caliphate. But that news comes at a terrible price. At least 23 journalists have been murdered by Islamic State militants from Syria to Iraq, Turkey and France. Islamic State leaders want to control all information leaving and entering their proclaimed territory and eliminate anyone that undermines that ambition.

"They have closed down the narrative space, scaring journalists away," said Charlie Winter, formerly a senior research associate at Georgia State University, who studies IS communications strategies. "IS uses the targeting to produce a vacuum," then tries to fill that vacuum with its own "news." Islamic State has set up its own Al-Bayan radio station and a sophisticated distribution network for its newsletter, *Al-Naba*, according to Winter and other IS-watchers. In the Iraqi city of Mosul, it has established dozens of news kiosks that distribute flash drives with videos and written content.

"It is working towards an information monopoly . . . where satellite television doesn't penetrate, where the internet isn't accessible," Winter told CPJ. "But it is not there yet and it is actually quite far away from that." Its censorship method for controlling information leaving its territory is binary: Work with us or die.

Anyone who pulls out a smartphone to photograph or record risks arrest and execution, according to journalists and residents who have fled the area. But there is still a hard core of clandestine residents willing to risk their lives to document how their region is being ruled.

"There is a black hole of information coming out with pinpricks of light from activists who are inside," Winter added. He pointed to such journalist collectives as Raqqa is Being Slaughtered Silently (RBSS) and Eye on the Homeland.

Ahmed Abd al-Qader is one of those points of light. He helped found Eye on the Homeland, an anonymous collective of reporters and activists formed to deliver news from areas where independent reporting is suppressed. He knows that any reporter caught by IS is marked for death. Islamic State killed his brother and has tried to assassinate him twice.

"A lot of people who try to report on them are executed in public," he said. A video was circulated in 2015 of two men "confessing" to working for RBSS and identifying themselves as Faisal Hussain al-Habib and Bashir Abduladhim al-Saado. The video ends with the men being tied to tree trunks and shot. Though RBSS, a hidden citizen journalist group formed after IS took over Raqqa in 2014, denied the men worked for the organization, the message to everyone inside and outside Raqqa was clear.

The public executions followed attempts at coercion to unearth journalists. The father and adopted brother of one RBSS member were held as hostages to coerce the reporters to surrender to IS. They did not, and both relatives were killed.

Abd al-Qader personally knows the price for crossing IS. He says IS has tried to kill him twice, even after he fled Syria for the relative safety of neighboring Turkey. "Daesh," he said, referring to IS by the name often used by its critics, "targeted me in Turkey and killed my brother because we exposed it as a terrorist organization . . . and the animosity of local people towards them." He apologized for not being more articulate about the events, as he was still recovering after having been shot in the face in June 2016 and speaks with difficulty. He recalled how IS agents killed his brother and fellow Eye on the Homeland member Ibrahim Abd al-Qader, along with their colleague Fares Hamadi, in an apartment in the southeast Turkey city of Urfa in 2015, shattering any illusion that exile might bring safety.

That IS would extend its deadly enforcement of censorship beyond its immediate territory comes as no surprise to Abdel Aziz al-Hamza, a founding member of RBSS, which received CPJ's International Press Freedom Award in 2015 for its work in Syria. "Everyone who is known to be working with us moved to Europe . . . because we can't consider Turkey safe," al-Hamza, who lives in exile in Europe, observed.

More than 7,000 miles away in Mexico, a handful of brave regional journalists feel much the same way. Mexico may boast of a vibrant democracy and economy, yet vast parts of the country are plagued by organized crime and corrupt local governments. A federal prosecutor's office to investigate crimes against freedom of expression and a federal protection mechanism have been largely ineffective, and both mainstream media reporters and bloggers are still being killed with total impunity for crossing the cartels.

In fact, many journalists don't even know where the cartel will draw its censorship line on any given day. Sometimes they want gang-related violence played down, and sometimes they want it reported, depending on how they think it reflects on them. "So the vulnerability that journalists experience usually comes from the fact that they sometimes don't know what they can cover and what they cannot cover," said Javier Garza, a journalist and former newspaper editor based in northern Mexico. The process of trying to determine what is off-limits has sometimes become absurd: Though circumstances have changed, and in some ways have further deteriorated, as far back as 2010 the daily *El Diario* threw up its hands and asked the cartels in the city of Ciudad Juárez what it could publish.

"You are the de facto authorities in this city, since our legitimate representatives have been unable to prevent our colleagues from being killed," the newspaper noted in an editorial that made world headlines.

Things have not improved much since then, except that journalists now sometimes get lists of censored topics to guide them.

"I recently met with a reporter from Tamaulipas, which is one of the states where organized crime exercises the most violence against the media, and they just picked up a list of subjects that are totally off limits to the press," Garza said. "They can report on the day's homicide or the day's shootings, but they can't report, for example, on government corruption or the complicity of government officials with criminal bosses, or they cannot report on businesses that have ties to criminal groups, such as the sale of alcohol or prostitution or contraband, corruption in police forces, businesses that have ties to organized crime that take on government contracts, for example, you know? Those subjects are totally off-limits." (These restrictions are also covered in chapter 10, "Edited by Drug Lords," by Elisabeth Malkin.)

The result of violent censorship in these regions of Mexico, as in Syria, has been the creation of information vacuums. That's where bloggers and others thought social media could fill the void. The drug lords had other ideas.

First came the two mutilated bodies hung from a bridge in the border town of Nuevo Laredo in September 2011. According to media reports, the victims had posted criticism of a cartel on social media. The motives for the killings could not be proved.

But the cartels left no doubt in the next killing of a journalist who had turned to social media in the same city days later.

María Elizabeth Macías Castro's body was left with a note. Her severed head was posed with headphones near a computer keyboard. The note, which referred to the journalist's pen name, read: "Ok. Nuevo Laredo Live and social media, I am the Girl from Laredo and I am here because of my reports and yours . . . ZZZZ." The ZZZZ signature suggests a link to the Zetas drug cartel. The murder was the first of a social media journalist in Mexico documented by CPJ. That and the 2014 disappearance of a critical Facebook blogger in the same state of Tamaulipas again underscored the vulnerability of journalists and would-be journalists without the rule of law, irrespective of publishing platforms.

"That had a huge chilling effect," Garza said. "One anonymous Twitter guy, I mean, one of the most trusted, told me that they had to lower their profile, in a big way, after that happened, and be more circumspect about what they tweeted."

To fill the information void created by murder and intimidation, the cartels frequently co-opt and corrupt journalists within mainstream media in the regions they control. In that way, they can plant or kill news stories at will.

"When a drug cartel wants to make a show of words, they want the stories published about who they're killing, for example, or who they're kidnapping, or whatever, they can do that," Garza said. "When they want these to keep quiet, when they don't want to attract too much attention, then they resort to censorship."

Journalists based in the relative safety of Mexico City can parachute in and cover parts of the crime and corruption story, but they cannot provide the sustained local coverage gleaned from local knowledge that residents really need.

What are the remedies for murderous censorship in Mexico or any of the dozens of other U.N. member democracies such as the Philippines, Pakistan, Nigeria or Brazil where impunity in the killing of journalists is rampant, let alone in IS-held territory?

Part of the answer lies with local journalists themselves. In Mexico, journalists at risk have started working collectively, never traveling alone to crime scenes, taking countersurveillance measures and sharing information on threats, journalists say.

Periodistas de a Pie (Journalists on Foot), a group founded in 2007 as an initiative to improve journalism standards, has transformed itself into a safety network and now provides training for vulnerable reporters. At the national level, journalists argue that the media needs to pressure the government to provide effective protection for regional journalists (at the very least) by strengthening the office of the federal prosecutor for crimes against free expression, which has so far failed to turn the tide of journalist killings.

Colombia has had a protection mechanism in place since the early 2000s, and the number of journalist deaths has decreased. The project has been successful because journalists and civil society have been integral members of the mechanism from the beginning, providing authorities with timely information but also pressuring the government for individualized protection measures, such as emergency evacuation and bodyguards for vulnerable journalists.

Though there have been recent convictions in the killings of journalists in Colombia, critics of the country's protection mechanism say that authorities involved in the project need to conduct further investigation into all attacks and prosecute the perpetrators. The project succeeded because the media and local press freedom group Fundación para la Libertad de Prensa (FLIP) was able to pressure the government to provide bodyguards and security for vulnerable journalists and push for prosecutions of journalist killers.

On the international level, journalists and activists have put the issue of press censorship through murder on the agenda. In 2013, the United Nations designated November 2 as the International Day to End Impunity for Crimes against Journalists, and UNESCO has since published a guide to help individual countries establish their own journalist safety mechanisms.

In Garza's view, impunity is the key issue. "More journalists are getting attacked because people doing the attacks are not getting punished," he said. "I think, really, that's the essence of it."

The effectiveness of such international measures and national journalist safety initiatives remains to be seen. They are certainly not of much immediate help to the Syrian citizen-journalists dodging IS.

But there are ways in which the global press freedom and media development community can help Syrian journalist collectives. These range from financial and legal support for journalists who have fled Syria to providing journalism training and equipment.

Eye on the Homeland's Abd al-Qader needs news-gathering gear. "We don't have a lot of cameras that we can give the reporters to get the news," he says of those inside Syria. "When they lose their cameras, they can't replace them." He also needs satellite phones and communications equipment.

And RBSS, which received lots of media interest and some foreign funding as its story emerged back in 2014 and 2015, is running out of money. Al-Hamza has a day job in Berlin that enables him to work for RBSS, which needs editors and translators. Its last source of funding from a U.S. nongovernmental organization dried up in January 2016, and the organization has been strapped ever since.

Islamic State, with its macabre violence against journalists and extreme information control, may be an outlier in the censorship landscape, and it may not even endure as a political and military force. But the issue of violent censorship remains a daily reality for many news gatherers and opinion writers. Not all countries can replicate the Colombian safety model, which depends on bringing together journalist groups, civil society and the security forces with the common purpose of enforcing the rule of law and ending impunity.

If the killers of Avijit Roy and the other bloggers aimed to shut down speech, they have not fully succeeded—yet. Bangladesh has functioning state institutions, but impunity is still rampant. The successors of Avijit Roy are still largely silent. Those bloggers who have not fled are wary. The police have not caught the masterminds, said Mainul Islam Khan, a journalist and press freedom advocate. And the government response? "Government's top leaders have urged all to be more careful and conscious in their writing so that their writings do not hit any religious sentiments," he told CPJ.

Robert Mahoney is deputy executive director of the Committee to Protect Journalists and writes about press freedom issues. He has worked as a correspondent in Asia, Africa, the Middle East and Europe.

18. Being a Target

By Rukmini Callimachi

A Timbuktu resident walks past a room where he and other residents say al-Qaeda held European hostages at Mali's Ministry of Finance regional audit department.

(AP/Rukmini Callimachi)

T he convoy of cars flying al-Qaeda's black flag swept across northern Mali in 2012. Within weeks, it felt like a curtain had been drawn.

Over scratchy phone lines, I dialed and re-dialed the numbers of city officials, which usually rang unanswered. When someone occasionally picked up, they couldn't hear me. By the time the amputations began, many were too afraid to speak.

I had been the West Africa bureau chief for The Associated Press for less than a year when al-Qaeda seized and began to govern the largest slice of territory they had ever held. The sweep of desert under their control, which the terror network's North African branch held with the help of two allied groups, spanned the size of Afghanistan. It should have been a riveting story, except that I couldn't cover it: The branch of al-Qaeda that had seized the territory had bankrolled its rise to prominence by kidnapping foreigners for ransom. Soon after the group planted their black flag in the fabled desert outpost of Timbuktu, a Swiss woman—who had refused to evacuate—was abducted from her home.

For the next 10 months, I watched from more than a thousand miles away in neighboring Senegal as reports surfaced of women being flogged for refusing to wear the black veil. I did my best to describe how they destroyed the centuries-old mausoleums of Timbuktu, spending an afternoon trying, and failing, to confirm anything beyond the most basic details. "Are you sure they used a sledgehammer?" I yelled into the phone one afternoon. "Or was it a pickaxe?" Mostly, I threw up my hands.

If I'm honest with myself, I failed to cover the story both because it was too hard and because it was less exciting: Instead of being out in the field, I was stuck in my office, forced to report on a speakerphone.

I was schooled not by another journalist, but by a report put out by a human rights group. Beginning in the summer of 2012, Human Rights Watch researcher Corinne Dufka traveled to Bamako, the capital of Mali. She spent her days at the central bus station, waiting for the buses making the journey from Timbuktu, carrying fleeing residents who had witnessed the group's brutal rule. Her report was full of the details I longed to cover: How the terror group had banned music in all its forms, going so far as to outlaw cell phone jingles. She described how one young man frantically tried to hit the answer button on his phone when someone called him and the ringer played Malian music within earshot of the jihadists. He was beaten until he bled, her report said.

It was a watershed moment for me. Huge swaths of the world are now off limits to reporters. Much of Syria and Iraq, where the militant group Islamic State has built its caliphate, are no-go zones both because of the regular dangers of war and because reporters are now targets. So is much of Libya, where until recently Islamic State ran its most important "province." The area where we can operate in Afghanistan has progressively shrunk. And despite Western-backed or -funded military interventions, most of Somalia, much of northern Nigeria, chunks of Niger, Chad and Algeria remain areas of extreme risk for journalists.

And yet what happens inside those no-go areas has become more important than ever.

For the past three and a half years, I have been approaching the edges of territories held by terror groups, inching as close as I can to the line of control, metaphorically peeking over the sandbags. In Mali, I also eventually headed to the bus stop to await the fleet of GDF buses making the days-long journey from the heart of territory controlled by al-Qaeda. I, too, spoke to the passengers as they exited the bus, the women visibly relieved to no longer have to wear the suffocating veil.

And I got better at using the telephone in my office, learning to use the redial function. I kept a notepad next to my landline and tallied each call I made, telling myself I wouldn't give up until I had dialed the same number at least 20 times. The interviews would sometimes last less than a minute before the line went dead, forcing me to redial yet again. I begged each person I called to introduce me to someone else, so that each call became part of a daisy chain of interviews.

It was difficult, often tedious work, but it paid off in the first weeks of 2013, when France scrambled fighter jets over northern Mali, beginning a military intervention to flush out the jihadists. I reached the city of Timbuktu days after it had been freed, part of a wave of reporters who cascaded into town, filling every available hotel room. I was not the first to reach the fabled city, but I was the last journalist to leave, staying for more than a month, until the manager of my hotel informed me that I would need to start paying a 5,000-franc (around US$10) fee each day to pay the cook. "There are no other guests, so he's coming just for you," the manager reasoned.

Because I had spent so much time on bad phone lines covering the occupied city, I already knew it intimately before ever stepping foot on its sand-enveloped lanes. I headed to the branch of the Banque Malienne de Solidarité (BMA bank), which had acted as the headquarters of the Islamic police. I knew the jihadists had turned the city's once-chic boutique hotel into the seat of their Shariah court, and I headed there next. Residents pointed me to the garage where Abou Zeid, one of the top commanders of al-Qaeda in the Islamic Maghreb, responsible for kidnapping numerous Western hostages, had waited for a mechanic to fix his Toyota SUV, to the tax building where his men had typed out their set of edicts, and to the other municipal offices and private villas that had served as the infrastructure of their occupying government.

In each building, I found and collected dozens of pages left behind by al-Qaeda's men.

Those documents, totaling more than 5,000 pages of internal correspondence and ideological treatises, have formed the core of my understanding of al-Qaeda, and helped orient my insight into its offshoot, the Islamic State.

It was another way to peer over the sandbags, this time through the peephole of what they wrote to each other and about themselves.

I finally left Timbuktu in March 2013, and during the next two years, my focus shifted almost entirely to the Islamic State group. I struggled at first to find the metaphorical bus stop where I could interview the passengers leaving the territory under their control. I finally found it on the first of four trips to Iraq in 2015, in the tent cities that had sprung up on the edges of the northern town of Dohuk. It was there that the Yazidi minority, whose women had been targeted for enslavement by Islamic State, found refuge. I filled my days going tent to tent, speaking to dozens of women held by the terror group. They related the horrors of their captivity—the rapes that had by then already been reported by numerous news organizations, including my own. For me, those interviews were the most intimate of windows into the state of mind of the men claiming to be acting in the name of God. The women and girls described how their abusers used scripture to justify acts of sexual violence. They told me that the fighters described their rape as *ibada*, the

Arabic word for worship, and they described how the men holding them prayed before the rape, then took a shower and then prayed again, bookending the abuse in an act of religious devotion.

I was in Iraq on November 13, 2015, when my editor called me and asked me to rush to Paris.

I arrived the next day and it took me an hour and a half to drive the normally 40-minute distance between Charles de Gaulle Airport and my hotel, as we were forced onto side streets to avoid the barricades erected by the security forces hunting the surviving attackers who killed 130 at the Stade de France, cafes and the Bataclan theater. As their names were revealed, I joined the flocks of reporters going from street to street, knocking on the doors of former neighbors, a frustrating and mostly futile exercise.

It was then that I found the next peephole in the form of interrogation documents and court records, traveling by train to Brussels to pick up the first folder.

France has sent more fighters to Syria than any other Western country, and dozens have been arrested upon their return. In transcripts of hours-long interrogations conducted by France's Direction Generale de la Securite Interieure, the country's domestic intelligence unit, I was able to glimpse the outlines of a branch of the Islamic State dedicated to exporting terror abroad. In mid-2016, a source handed me a USB stick containing more than 100,000 pages of investigative documents, and I have been combing through them, using them as the spine of stories on how Islamic State mounted the machinery of terror in Europe. More recently, I have begun to collect similar interrogation records from Asia, showing the group's global reach.

I am never happier than when I am in the field, and I cannot help but read with longing the accounts of reporters who covered conflict years ago, when journalists were still considered off-bounds. It was only 20 years ago that Osama bin Laden welcomed an American TV crew inside a hut on a cold mountaintop in Afghanistan. I wonder if those opportunities will ever come again for Western reporters.

Until then, I'll keep on working as close as I can to the edges.

Rukmini Callimachi *is a three-time Pulitzer Prize finalist who covers the militant groups Islamic State and al-Qaeda for* The New York Times.

19. Fighting for the Truth

By Christiane Amanpour

Journalists face "an existential crisis, a threat to the very relevance and usefulness of our profession," says the author, pictured in 2014.

(CPJ)

N ever in a million years did I expect to find myself appealing for the freedom and safety of American journalists at home. Despite the hostile rhetoric of the U.S. presidential campaign, I hoped that after becoming president-elect, Donald Trump would change his approach to the press.

But I was chilled when among the first tweets Trump sent out after the election was about "professional protesters incited by the media." Though he later walked back the part about the protesters, he did not soften his stance about the media's incitement. Though we are not there yet, here's a postcard from the world: This is how it goes with authoritarians like Egypt's Abdel Fattah el-Sisi, Turkey's Recep Erdoğan, Russia's Vladimir Putin, the Ayatollahs, the Philippines' Rodrigo Duterte, et al.

International journalists know only too well: First, the media is accused of inciting, sympathizing and associating, then suddenly they find themselves accused of being full-fledged subversives and even terrorists. They end up in handcuffs, in cages in kangaroo courts, in prison—and then, who knows?

In late 2016, Turkey's Erdoğan, who has the ignominious distinction of running a country with more journalists behind bars than any other, told my Israeli colleague Ilana Dayan that he could not understand why anyone protested Trump's election in America; that it must mean they don't accept or understand democracy. He thinks America, like all great countries, needs a strongman to get things done. But what all great countries need is a free press and certainly not a strongman who wants to limit their ability to tell the truth. In fact, a great America requires a great, free and safe press.

Because journalism is under siege worldwide, we must appeal to protect the profession itself, including in the country whose free media has historically led the way. To do that, we must recommit to robust fact-based reporting without fear or favor on the issues. We cannot stand for being labeled crooked or lying or failing. We must stand up together, for divided, we will all fall.

The historian Simon Schama told me early on that the 2016 U.S. presidential campaign was not about just another election and that we could not treat it as one. After the election, he told me that if there were ever a time to celebrate, honor, protect and mobilize for press freedom and basic good journalism, it was now.

Like many people watching from overseas, I admit that I was shocked by the exceptionally high bar put before one candidate and the exceptionally low bar put before the other candidate. It appeared much of the media got itself into knots trying to differentiate between balance, objectivity, neutrality and, crucially, truth.

We cannot continue to give equal play to climate deniers as we do to those who rely on the fact that 99.9 percent of the empirical scientific evidence proves man-made climate change is occurring. I learned long ago, while covering the ethnic cleansing and genocide in Bosnia, never to equate victim with aggressor, never to create a false moral or factual equivalence, because then you are an accomplice to the most unspeakable crimes and consequences. I believe in being truthful, not neutral. And I believe we must stop banalizing the truth. We as journalists have to be prepared to fight especially hard for the truth in a world where the *Oxford English Dictionary* announced that "post-truth" was the notable word of 2016.

We also have to accept that we've had our lunch handed to us by the very same social media that we've so slavishly been devoted to. The winning candidate did a savvy end run around us and used it to go straight to the people with whatever version of the truth he chose. That end run was combined with the most incredible development ever—the tsunami of fake news sites, a.k.a. lies—that somehow people could not, would not, recognize, fact-check or disregard. One of the main writers of these false articles says people are getting dumber, just passing fake reports around without fact-checking. We need to ask whether technology has finally outpaced our human ability to keep up. Facebook needs to step up to stem the flow of fake news, and advertisers need to boycott the lying sites. The truth cannot be treated as a relative term.

Wael Ghonim, one of the fathers of the Arab Spring, which has also been dubbed the social media revolution, put it this way: "The same medium that so effectively transmits a howling message of change also appears to undermine the ability to make it. Social media amplifies the human tendency to bind with one's own kind. It tends to reduce complex social challenges to mobilizing slogans that reverberate in echo chambers of the like-minded rather than engage in persuasion, dialogue, and the reach for consensus. Hate speech and untruths appear alongside good intentions and truths."

Given the array of challenges facing the free press around the world, including in its historical bastion, the U.S., we as journalists face an existential crisis, a threat to the very relevance and usefulness of our profession. Now, more than ever, we need to commit to real reporting across a real nation, a real world in which journalism and democracy are in mortal peril, including by foreign powers such as Russia, paying to churn out and place false news and hacking into democratic systems in the U.S. and allegedly in crucial German and French elections, and hacking into the institutions of many other countries, too.

We must also fight against a post-values world and against this "elitist" backlash that we're all bending over backward to accommodate. Since when are American values elitist? They are not left or right values. They are not rich or poor values, not the forgotten-man values. Like many foreigners I have learned that they are universal. They are the values of the humblest to the most exalted Americans. They form the very fundamental foundation of the U.S. and are the basis of its global leadership. They are brand America. They are America's greatest export and gift to the world.

Lying and promoting lies is not an American value. Yet the 2016 presidential election actually embraced so much that is untrue and created an unprecedented paradigm: Very few ever imagined that so many Americans conducting their sacred duty in the sanctity of the voting booth, with their secret ballot, would be angry enough to ignore the wholesale vulgarity of language, the sexual predatory behavior, the deep misogyny, the bigoted and insulting views and the deliberate falsehoods that were sometimes followed by lies claiming they had never been said, even when they were recorded on video. Governor Mario Cuomo said you campaign in poetry and govern in prose. Perhaps the opposite will be true this time around. If not, we must all fight as journalists to defend and protect the unique value system that makes these United States, and with which it seeks to influence the world.

After the election, there was a "Heil, victory" meeting in Washington, D.C., which represented a move about as far from traditional American values as you can get. Why aren't there more stories about the dangerous rise of the far right here and in Europe? Since when did neo-Nazism and anti-Semitism stop being a litmus test in this country? We must fight against normalization of the unacceptable.

A week before the heated Brexit referendum in the U.K., the gorgeous, young, optimistic, idealistic, compassionate minister of parliament, Jo Cox, a Remainer, was shot and stabbed to death by a maniac yelling, "Britain first." At his trial, the court was told the accused had researched information on the SS and the KKK. Her husband, Brendan, now raising their two tiny toddlers, expanded for me on an op-ed he'd written: "Political leaders and people generally must embrace the responsibility to speak out against bigotry. Unless the center holds against the insidious creep of extremism, history shows how quickly hatred is normalized. What begins with biting your tongue for political expediency, or out of social awkwardness, soon becomes complicity with something far worse. Before you know it, it's already too late."

What are we to do? Beyond reporting the truth, and not normalizing the unacceptable, we must ensure that the war of attrition in this country comes to an end. The presidential election was very close, but it illustrated a sharp divide. And it both revealed and tapped into a remarkably deep well of anger. Are we in the media going to keep whipping up that war, or are we going to take a deep breath and have a reset?

These things not only matter for the future of the U.S. and the country's media. They matter to us out there abroad. For better or for worse, the U.S. is the world's only superpower, and its political and media examples are emulated and rolled out across the world. We, the media, can contribute either to a more functional system or to deepening the political dysfunction.

Which world do we want to leave our children?

American politics has driven itself into poisonous partisan and paralyzing corners, where political differences are criminalized, where the zero-sum game means that in order for me to win, you have to be destroyed. What happened to compromise and common ground? That same dynamic has infected powerful segments of the American media as it has in Egypt, Turkey and Russia, where journalists have been pushed into political partisan corners, delegitimized and accused of being enemies of the state. Journalism itself has become weaponized. We cannot allow that to happen.

We all have a huge amount of work to do, investigating wrongdoing, holding power accountable, enabling decent government, defending basic rights, actually covering the world. As a profession, we must fight for what is right. We must fight for our values. Because bad things do happen when good people do nothing.

In the words of the great civil rights leader Congressman John Lewis: "Young people and people not so young have a moral obligation and a mission and a mandate to get in good trouble."

So, let's go out and make some trouble. Let's fight to remain relevant and useful. Let's reveal lies for what they are, and fight for the truth. Because the future of the world depends on it.

Christiane Amanpour is CNN's chief international correspondent, anchor of the network's global affairs program "Amanpour," a senior adviser to the Committee to Protect Journalists and a goodwill ambassador for press freedom and safety at UNESCO. In November 2016, she received CPJ's Burton Benjamin Memorial Award for her extraordinary and sustained achievement in the cause of press freedom. This report was adapted from her acceptance speech.

Index